Boynton Dreams

Fabian Hernandez

Contents

Chapter One

SEPTEMBER 10th, 2001

It was another humid morning in Florida, and the line at the Weiss & Fletcher bookstore cafe stretched outside the door. It was the largest bookstore on the east coast of America. From the entryway, the shelves looked like they were stocked with millions of books from every genre imaginable. Oddballs, punks, and intellects from all walks of life commonly convened at that store, shunning themselves from the chaos of the outside world for a moment of focus and clarity. The wide area created a sense of privacy for those loners and unlimited opportunities for the kleptomaniacs.

The most prestigious target for thieves was the music section. It was where the latest CDs, DVDs, box sets, and other desirable items were sold. In a place where there were no security measures, the last line of defense against thievery was dedicated workers.

Other than a few middle-aged managers, most of the store's workers were recent high school graduates with few life plans. They were wanderers, weirdos, and slackers who only cared about collecting a paycheck. Because of their carelessness, people were always stealing from that store.

The young man responsible for overseeing the music section was an outsider who always wore a sad look on his face, except when he was drunk. In the company training course for theft prevention, it was made clear to him that he was "the protector of revenue on the frontlines of surveillance." Although he could not care less about corporate revenues, he at least tried to show his managers that he cared about his job… when they were looking.

On a morning that was no different than the rest, he was organizing the returns and new-release albums that were stored behind the register table. He despised the lingering process because it constantly reminded him of how miserable his life was.

As always, his portly supervisor stood nearby to micromanage his work. She was the Regional Manager of the store who never missed an opportunity to lecture him on the importance of organization. "There is no such thing as being too organized," she said in a pestering tone as he slaved away. But each time the music attendant heard it, he drifted into his demented thoughts, fantasizing about pelleting her with CDs and DVDs until she was unconscious. But in reality, he just kept his head down and stacked the shelves until she left.

For that young man, the only perk of the job was being surrounded by music. It was an enriching distraction from his reality, with thousands of artists keeping him inspired throughout the shift. His deeply embedded appreciation of underground music and punk rock made him a vicious critic of the popular genres. But occasionally, he expanded his musical boundaries by discovering something new and groundbreaking.

In the afternoon, there were a few customers on the floor browsing the CDs. Over by the listening section, an incognito man wearing shades and a hat was listening to every album on the display wall. He stood there wearing the giant headphones while bopping his head to the featured artists of the week. The second customer was a young Hispanic with dark hair and olive-colored skin. He was scouring the "urban" section for new releases, rapidly flipping through the CDs. The third customer, a female senior citizen, walked around the jazz section for a half hour, drinking coffee and pecking away at a scone. The music attendant noticed the track of crumbs she left on the floor.

"Fucking bitch," he said to himself.

After the new releases were properly shelved, the worker grabbed one of each, twelve in total, and placed them into a large bag behind the register. Then he grabbed various box sets and another handful of CDs from under the register and also placed them in the bag. When he raised his head from behind the counter, the senior citizen was coldly staring at him.

"Yes, miss? How can I help you?" said the soft-spoken worker.

"Do you have 'My Favorite Things' by John Coltrane? It's my husband's favorite, and I want to surprise him for his birthday. I looked everywhere, and I couldn't find it," said the octogenarian northerner.

"Sure, I can find out for you on the computer. You said Coltrane?" replied the attendant.

"I couldn't have said it any clearer… John," responded the rude woman as she adjusted her glasses to read his name tag.

John, the music section worker, ignored her attitude. He became accustomed to dealing with entitled snowbirds. They were everywhere in west Boynton, pestering retail and service-industry workers with their impatient demands.

"I'm sorry, ma'am, but the album isn't available in this store. It is available in Boca if you want to go there to pick it up," said John. He was already anticipating her smug response.

"Uh, I'm eighty-one years old. Do you think I have the energy to drive all the way to Boca? This place never has… anything… I'm looking for. How do you expect to make any money if customers can't find... what they're looking for?" complained the woman in her thick accent while pausing between moments of dementia.

John wasn't in the mood to argue with the woman or accommodate her. He just gave her a blank, emotionless stare and said, "I'm sorry. There's nothing I can do."

"Of course, have a good day," said the rude woman as she walked out of the music section.

After she left, John walked around the entire music section to clean garbage left in the aisles. He arrived at the urban section, where the Hispanic customer was still browsing. After picking up the snowbird's coffee cup, he looked at his watch to note the amount of time the young man had been there.

After searching the rest of the aisles, John returned to the register where the Hispanic customer was waiting. Without saying a word, he handed John a stack of CDs. John ran them through the tag-deactivating machine and placed them in the overstuffed Weiss & Fletcher bag. After adding the customer's CDs, it was full to the brim. John realized the excessive weight of the bag and put it in a second bag for additional support.

The customer waited until John placed the giant bag on the register counter. At that point, the customer grabbed the bag and also took notice of the weight. Still, he just nodded at John, adjusted his Arnette sunglasses from his scalp to his eyes, and left the music section with the bag.

"Have a good day, sir," was all John said.

At the same time, one of the workers from the café arrived to talk to John. She was a gutter punk, a Midwest runaway who was completely infatuated with him. Her name was Angelica Wilding. Other than a handful of belongings in a room she rented, the barista job was all she had.

"Heeey! How come you didn't come by during your break?" Angelica asked John in a squeaky voice.

"I went to take a little smoke break. I saw the line was huge, so I knew you couldn't come with me," replied John.

"I know! You saw that? There was this lady who kept ordering the Caramel Frappuccino. Every time I handed it to her, she would taste it and then say that I wasn't making it right. She stood there for nearly ten minutes arguing with me until she realized she meant to ask for a Caramel Macchiato," said the overly excited clinger.

"So, is this your break?" asked John with a flirtatious undertone. He held a smug look on his face while looking squarely into her eyes. It was the look he always gave her when he wanted to have sex.

Five minutes later, they were humping in the storage closet by the employee lounge. John was penetrating her from the back with his hand on her mouth to mask the moaning. They'd had intercourse more than fifty times in that closet without ever getting caught. For John, it was friendly sex with no emotional attachment. For Angelica, it was more than that.

After his shift ended, John left the store and walked to his beige Ford Escort. It was old and ugly, but the only car he could afford. He entered through the front passenger door because the driver's door did not open. After scooching to the driver's seat, he put the key into the ignition and tried three times to turn on the engine. On the fourth try, the car started. John then lit a cigarette and drove out of the Boynton Commons parking lot.

There was little hope in John Thibault's stormy life. The daily drive home was a strong reminder of that. The interior of the car was mangled, and there was garbage scattered everywhere. The only bright side was the sub-woofer and large speaker that allowed John to tune out his misery with loud punk rock like Rancid and Less-than-Jake.

John pulled into a new apartment complex that was built adjacent to the Florida Turnpike. He parked the car, grabbed his bookbag, and walked to the apartment he shared with his mother, her new husband, and his younger brother.

John found his mother sleeping on the couch with a half-finished bottle of wine resting on the coffee table. It was always a tormenting sight to see, but he could never scorn his mother for her behavior. Instead, he covered her with a quilt to make sure she was comfortable.

He put down his book bag and leaped on his bed to reach the blinds string. He wrapped it around his hand and pulled it to let light enter the room. To his surprise, the Hispanic customer from earlier in the day was pressing his face against the window while holding a blunt in his mouth.

"Fuck! You scared the shit out of me, Guapos," said John. "Go to the front."

John's best friend nodded his head, picked up the overstuffed Weiss & Fletcher bag, and walked to the front door. When he opened it, he saw Alexis Garcia holding the loot from the heist they pulled.

"Whoa! Shit! Guapos! I didn't realize how full the bag was," said John as Alexis walked inside the apartment.

"I swore this was going to break on the way out. I was shitting a brick the entire time," said Alexis. "I was ready to run the fuck out of there if anything happened." John laughed at his friend's creative paranoia.

Alexis saw John's mother on the couch and became overwhelmed with pity. She was not the same vibrant woman that he once knew; the gym rat, the involved P.T.A member, the one who would drive them to baseball practice every day and the movies on the weekend. He walked quietly to the room to not disturb her, but she woke up anyway.

"John, honey, can you please get me some water?" she said.

"Sure, Mom. Alexis is here," he informed her.

"Hi, honey! Tell your mother I said hello," she muttered with her eyes still closed.

"Will do, Betsy!" replied Alexis from John's room.

Alexis sat on John's bedroom couch and turned the overstuffed bag upside down to remove its items. Out came thirty CDs, twenty DVDs, and three expensive boxsets. He separated a few personal items that were his to keep and left the rest for John to sort. After that, Alexis sat back and continued to smoke his blunt while observing the sports memorabilia on the wall. It was John's collection that he'd admired ever since they were kids. Every item was displayed in a specific order, on a plaque, or in a protective case.

There were baseball collectibles, such as a signed Nolan Ryan picture of "the bloody lip" incident with Bo Jackson and a signed

Mickey Mantle portrait. There were also hockey collectibles everywhere because John's heritage was French-Canadian, and he was a die-hard Florida Panthers fan. The team was five years removed from their only Stanley Cup appearance and was currently in last place in the eastern conference. John's mood was dramatically influenced by the team's success and failure.

The door opened. John walked in with two cold beers. He handed one to Alexis and took the blunt for a few hits. He then opened the window to evade the smell and settled on the edge of his bed to review the stolen items.

"Let's see what we got here," he said. "The new Rancid, the new Blink, and Sublime's Greatest Hits... What did you get? Let me guess... something from the urban aisle."

"I didn't get this Bone Thugs in the urban aisle. And I think this Wu-Tang was in the easy listening section," sarcastically replied Alexis.

"That's a lot of fucking CDs. I think we're almost ready," said John after observing the loot. "What do you think?"

"How many bags are there?" asked Alexis.

"This one, and I've got seven in the closet. One more, and I think we'll be good for the Swap Shop," said John. "You think you're good for one more trip?"

"Dude, this was all my idea. Let's do it," replied Alexis before taking a hit.

"Oh… this was all my idea… I'm Guapos… I'll kill you if you take my idea…," mocked John in a low and depressing tone.

"Yeah, that's right, motherfucker," replied Alexis with

intensity. "I'm the mastermind."

"I think we should schedule it for this weekend," suggested John while grabbing the blunt from his tense friend.

"What do you mean? The heist or the Swap Shop?" asked Alexis.

"Both, I guess. You can come in tomorrow for the last heist, and we'll do Swap Shop on Saturday," said John.

"Motherfucker, I have a lot of shit to do this week. I've got a final today, tomorrow, and two more on Friday. Can't do it until next week," affirmed Alexis.

"Oh, I forgot, Guapos and school, so sorry, no disrespect, Meng. Don't want to upset mama and papa," continued John with his friendly mockery of the Hispanic culture.

"Go fuck yourself," replied Alexis before remembering another university task. "Wait a minute, what's the date today?"

"Uh, the date is September 10th… Why?" replied John.

"Fuck, I have to fill out a survey for extra credit, and it's due today before eight. I gotta go," said Alexis before standing up to exit the room. He held the stack of stolen CDs with his right arm while walking to the door.

"I'll call you later. We'll figure this out," said Alexis.

On his way out, Alexis noticed a picture of their old baseball team hanging by the door. In the middle were the two friends at twelve years old, and their coach, John's father, was standing on the side.

"Was this from that day?" asked Alexis.

"Yup," replied John.

"Why do you have that shit up? You didn't hang it in your old room. Isn't it… kind of a shitty reminder," said the brutally honest friend.

"Not entirely. Remember your home run?" asked John.

"Every fucking day. I'll see you later, man," replied Alexis before walking out of the apartment.

Chapter Two

John returned to work the next day at 7 a.m. in dreadful anticipation of a double shift. He sat in the parking lot to rest his eyes for a few more seconds before leaving the car. It was a moment of the day that he used to mentally prepare himself for all the people he would encounter. He then took a final hit of weed and held in the smoke until he stepped out of the car.

By 8:20 a.m., he had already finished organizing the music section. All the while, he sensed that something was different. The environment was too docile, and none of the other staff had arrived. But as he was taking the books that he found in the music section back to their appropriate sections of the store, the Regional Manager arrived. She was in a frenzy, unable to contain her emotions.

"Tanisha, what's wrong?" said another tattooed worker.

"Didn't you hear the news? We're being attacked. A bunch of planes are being hijacked all over the country," replied Tanisha.

John pretended like he was working and couldn't hear. But he heard everything. He continued to put away books in the New Age section until Tanisha arrived to mention the attack.

"Hey, John," she said with watery eyes.

"Hey, Tanisha. What's up? Are you okay?" he asked.

"I'm not sure," she said before sucking snot. After wiping the liquids from her face, she continued. "I was on my way to work when the radio announced that some plane in New York had been hijacked. Then ten minutes later, another plane was hijacked. And then reports came out of a third airplane. Nobody knows what's happening, and I'm a little scared."

"Oh, God. What do we do? Is there an emergency plan for the store?" asked John, who only wanted to get out of work.

"Yes, that's what I'm going to review right now because this feels like an emergency... But I'm surprised to see you here. I thought you were off today," said Tanisha.

"I thought I was working," replied John.

"No, not today. Eddie is working music today," confirmed Tanisha.

"Oh, well, let him know that I already organized the music and movies," said John.

"Will do. You stay safe out there," added Tanisha.

"I promise I will," replied John to mock her overdramatic reaction to the situation.

John left work feeling happy as a free bird. Just when he thought the day was going to suck, he found out that he didn't have to be there. All he wanted to do was get high, have a few beers, and watch movies the rest of the morning. He got in his car and turned on the ignition on the first attempt. As he was picking out a CD from an enormous CD album, he noticed the radio station talking about the alleged hijackings.

"...I can't believe what we're hearing. As of right now, two airplanes have been hijacked, American Airlines Flight 77 from Washington and Flight 11 from Boston have been hijacked. It appears that both flights have re-routed, and we're not sure where they're headed...

"What the fuck?" said John as he listened anxiously. A minute later, Alexis called.

"What the fuck is happening, bro?" said John as he answered the phone.

"We're fucking under attack. I came to class, but I think everything was canceled. The door was locked, and none of the other students heard from the professor. I've been listening to this shit all morning on Stern. It's fucking crazy… What are you doing?"

"Nothing anymore, I came to work, but my boss said I wasn't scheduled for the day. So, you wanna smoke?" replied John.

"Fuck yeah! Go to my place. Nobody's there except Leo," replied Alexis.

"Oh, shit… this is going to be funny. I'll see you there," said John.

Alexis also lived in west Boynton but under different circumstances than John. Alexis's parents were doctors who had been married for thirty years. Their home was new, big, and on an acre of land. He was spoiled by middle-class standards, always driving a new car and spending his parent's money on the finest weed in town. His parents also paid for his college, an opportunity that Alexis tried not to waste.

Both of their cars arrived at the house at the same time, just after the first plane crashed into the north tower of the World Trade Center. Like everyone else in America, they were also wired to the media's depiction of the events. Although little had been confirmed, it definitively felt like America was being attacked by foreign terrorists.

"What the fuck is happening, bro!?" said Alexis as he stepped out of his car wearing his shades.

"It's war, man. We're at fucking war," replied John. "Fat boy is here?"

"Yeah, that's his new truck," replied Alexis as he pointed to the shiny, red Ford Ranger.

"Nice, maybe he can sell me some weed. I'm running low," replied John as they walked through the garden to the front door. "I can't stay too long. I'm having lunch with my dad," he added.

"How is old Luke?" replied Alexis.

"Man, he's insane. He fucking hates me," replied John with a depressed tone.

"What did you do this time?" asked Alexis. He was all too familiar with the dynamics of John's relationship with his father. Ever since they were kids, he had a front-row seat to the family turmoil.

"I told him he was drinking too much. Last time I saw him, he was so fucked-up that he could barely talk," replied John.

Every time John arrived at the double doors, he awed at the home's beauty. Everything was pristine, and he was scared to touch Mrs. Garcia's furniture. The tile sparkled like a newly waxed car, and the oak furniture gave the house a permanent earthy aroma.

They hustled up the wooden stairs to Alexis' room to watch the news on the television. Along the way, they both noticed a distinct smell coming from the second floor. Alexis followed the smell to his bedroom, opened the door, and saw his older brother blowing gravity-bong hits out the window. He was a weed dealer and was in the process of bagging two pounds that he had just received from California.

"Did you see what happened in New York?" he said after blowing smoke out the window.

"I heard everything on Stern," said Alexis as he watched the news on the television while standing. "Shit, the whole fucking building is on fire," he commented.

Meanwhile, John sat on the other side of Alexis' bed to inspect Leo's large bag of weed.

"Whoa, these are some nice nugs, fat boy," said John to get a hyper-aggressive reaction out of Leo. The two had an unusual relationship that consisted of insults, sarcasm, and angry outbursts.

"Hey, fuck you, you French motherfucker. Who you calling fat!?" expressed Leo as he jumped off the floor and pinned John on the bed to deliver rib punches. Leo was stocky, muscular, and strong as a horse. He had a playful demeanor, the type that sometimes made him look like an idiot. But his parent's commitment to expensive schooling left him with a high level of intelligence and intuition that few knew existed.

"Oh shit, check this out!" said Alexis while taking a hit and watching the television. He reacted to the second airplane hitting the south tower of the World Trade Center.

Nobody could move from the horror that was unfolding. They watched with their mouths open. Something that nobody believed would ever happen again did actually happen. America had been attacked.

"Those fucking Punjabis!?" expressed Alexis, who clearly knew that the term *Punjabi* referenced people of Indian culture. He just chose to say something foolish while puffing his chest like a Neanderthal.

"I can't fucking believe this," said Leo before taking two more gravity bong hits. He then re-packed the bowl and allowed John and Alexis to take hits. They each inhaled massive amounts of marijuana smoke from the plastic soda bottle as the September 11th events unfolded.

They watched the television in silence, each one generating unique emotions from the horrific sight. Alexis looked like he was ready to fight someone. Leo was too high to speak. And John was experiencing something out of the ordinary. Like the others, he was angry. But, at the same time, an unexpected wildfire was sparking in his mind.

John left the Garcia house at noon to meet his father for lunch. Thanks to Leo's gravity bong hits, he was baked out of his skull and looking forward to a good meal. They were meeting at the family's restaurant that was owned by John's grandfather, Jean Luke Thibault, an immigrant from Montreal who was a successful real estate broker in Broward County in the sixties. That success led him to form partnerships and open five successful restaurants in Broward and Palm Beach County. Technically, John's family was ridiculously wealthy, but he never saw a dime of that anymore.

The Yellow Tail restaurant was located on Boynton Beach's Intracoastal Waterway, just off Ocean Avenue. John's father was waiting for him at the deck bar, drinking a Miller Light and eating oysters. He was a familiar face at the restaurant because he used to be a manager. But his drinking, drug use, and violent temper ruined that opportunity. At present, he was out of work, broke, and somewhat exiled from the family.

"Hey, Luke! Do you want me to get you another beer?" said the young, blonde bartender.

"Sure, baby. Hook me up," replied Luke Thibault. His accent still muttered the remnants of a Canadian immigrant.

Luke's head was down as he prepared another oyster with lemon and salt. He did not know that John was standing behind him, gathering the confidence to start a conversation.

"Dad," was all he said in a low tone. His father did not hear, so John said again, a little louder, "Dad!"

Luke finally heard and turned halfway around, never looking his son in the eyes.

"Hey, Johnny. Good to see you. Here, I saved you a seat," he said.

John immediately noticed how much weight his father had gained since the last time they met. Also, his face was flushed from stress and high blood pressure. He fronted a presentable look with a pressed collared shirt and sleeves rolled up to flaunt the old Rolex. But John knew better. He knew that his father was not in a good place financially or emotionally.

Luke continued to eat with his head down as John looked through the menu. The bartender saw him and said, "Hi, Johnny! Haven't seen you here in a while... what are you drinking?"

"I'll have a Miller Light," he replied.

They sat in silence for a couple of minutes as John waited for his beer. He never wanted to say anything wrong to his father for fear of triggering his anger. Instead of talking or saying something foolish, they both watched the television to continue hearing details of the terrorist attack.

"Can you believe these Arabs? They're fucking animals, killing all those innocent people. Today is a very sad day, son," said Luke, who had heard enough of the miserable news. "I'm tired of seeing this… Hey! Jenny! Can you turn on SportsNet? I think the Marlins are playing a day game today."

Jenny, the bartender, grabbed the control and changed the channel.

"There you go… thanks, love," said Luke. "So, how's your brother?" he asked John.

"Vincent is good. He's bar-backing at The Brew House. I hardly see him anymore," replied John.

"Well, good. It's good that he's working. How about you? Still at the bookstore?"

"Yep," was all John replied.

At that moment, a commercial played on the television for a local sports museum in Boca Raton, starring its pudgy owner. He was walking the museum grounds while showing off all the signed sports memorabilia that he owned. It was a remarkable collection, with some items available for sale and other items solely for display.

The end of the commercial was reserved for the museum's crown jewel, a 1910 Honus Wagner baseball card that was worth millions. It was the most expensive baseball card in the world. The owner stood by the display while inviting sports lovers to the store. All the while, John could not take his eye off the card.

"That guy is such an asshole. Herb Bowman… he tried to sue your grandpa a few times back in the nineties over some property business deals. He's a scumbag who owes a lot of people money," expressed Luke.

"How much is that card worth?" asked John.

"Just over two million, I think," replied Luke.

For John, that was an immense figure to rationalize. There was a peaceful numbness that overcame his entire body after hearing the card's worth. The feeling that he had experienced earlier was erupting into vivid revelation.

"Have you seen your mother? Is she getting better?" asked Luke as John got out of his train of thought.

"No," replied John in a resentful tone. "She's still crazy, and it's probably not getting any better."

"Well, your mom was always crazy. So, don't worry. It's not all your fault," replied Luke before chugging the rest of his beer.

He put down the glass with enough force to alarm the bartender. As a result, John's face turned pale. Little outbursts like that were usually the first sign of his dad turning into a lunatic. John did not say another word. At that point, he knew it was best to avoid talking with his father.

Every time a boat passed along the Intracoastal, Luke stared at its glamor. They reminded him of a better time when he had his own boat, his own house, and his family.

"Hey, do you remember the boat? You kids loved that thing… gotta get us another boat," was all he said while chewing his fries.

For the rest of lunch, they sat at the bar and ate their food in cold silence. After the putrid history they shared, it was a miracle that John still wanted to make time for his father. That was because nothing meant more to him than his family, no matter what.

Chapter Three

One week had passed since the twin towers collapsed. While the country was trying to process its new sense of vulnerability, life in Boynton Beach quickly returned to normal. John returned to work, and Alexis finished his exams. Because he was between semesters, the boys planned to use the free time to conduct another heist.

Alexis waited in the parking lot of the Weiss and Fletcher Bookstore for Tanisha, the manager, to leave for lunch. Knowing her patterns was essential. It allowed Alexis to conduct the heist with little worry. She left the store exactly at 1:00 p.m., queueing Alexis to take a last hit of weed and enter the store.

It was their eighth heist overall, and the process was always the same. Alexis would enter the store through the café doors and order a tall coffee. After adding cream and sugar, he would proceed to the music section that was in the back of the store. He traversed through the outer aisles to draw little attention to himself. Along the way, he walked by the Health section, the Women's Studies section, the Children's section, the sports books and exercise books, the bathrooms, and the World History section, all the while going undetected by other workers.

The store didn't have security cameras either. That meant that he and John shared the risk because the only way to determine theft was through the inventory count. Because John was an employee and Alexis was not, John was the only one who could get investigated. But with the store's excessive theft problem, they operated under the assumption that the heist was undetectable.

Alexis always entered the music section without ever

addressing or looking at John. By that time, John already had a bag of loot carefully prepared. He would grab some items for personal enjoyment and hand them to John at the register. John scanned each item to deactivate the theft-prevention barcode and then placed everything in the bag. He handed Alexis the monstrous bags of stolen goods, and Alexis would swiftly leave the music section.

The shortest distance from the music section to the front door was through the center aisle. It was a straight shot, about two hundred feet away. From the moment Alexis stepped out of the music section, he became nervous and started sweating. But no matter how much burning sweat landed in his eyes, he kept them locked on the front door.

There were two possibilities that Alexis feared could happen. The first was that the bag could break. It was filled to the top and heavier than any single paper bag should tolerate, hence John's double-bag technique. The second possibility was being stopped by one of the employees. He knew that he wouldn't go down without a fight, adding assault to the list of crimes. He often imagined a chaotic situation where he would knock out one of the employees before sprinting to the door, knocking over people and display cases along the way.

On that day, the Customer Service attendant was busy helping two schoolgirls order a copy of Johnny Tremaine. Alexis maintained a casual pace to avoid being noticed, counting the steps in his head to ease his nerves. The bags were massive, and he was aware of how awkward he looked holding them.

After counting the thirteenth step, he knew he'd gotten past the first checkpoint. The last checkpoint was the register aisle. As always, there were only two people working the registers. The middle-aged woman with a lifeless scowl on her face was attending to a customer while the husky, bearded man was scanning returned items back into the system. Alexis passed them without a problem, briskly walking through the front door. He put the bags in the trunk of his car and drove off the parking lot.

That evening, John and Alexis met again at the Garcia house to review the final details of the next day's sale. It was eleven p.m., and they were drinking beers in Alexis' room while smoking weed out the open window. Alexis was sitting on his loveseat while John sat on the wood floor against the wall. They were cutting off labels and dividing all the items into sections.

Alexis was enjoying the moment. He was excited because he knew they had a great product to sell. The same couldn't be said about John. He was distracted, quieter than usual. Alexis noticed but continued to feed his friend alcohol in celebration of the moment.

"Well, fuck-boy, here's to tomorrow. This is some real felon shit that we've pulled off. Hopefully, we can make a lot of money... cheers!" said a proud Alexis.

"Cheers, bro," replied John.

They touched cans, and Alexis proceeded to chug both of his beers, one after the other. He widened his glottis and hardly spilled a drop as it poured down his gullet. Then he unleashed a monstrous burp into the air. John found it humorous, but he barely reacted.

"What the fuck is wrong, man!? You gotta get into your zone! It's game time! Tomorrow we gotta get rid of this shit and make as much money as possible. It's been fun and all, but I don't want to do this anymore. If we keep it up, we're gonna get caught, and there goes my acceptance into grad school. Snap the fuck out of it!" lectured Alexis.

"I'm good, bro. I hear you. I only wanted to do this until I could afford a new car. You know I need this," said John.

"I'm going to waste the money on a trip to Europe. You should think about coming with me. Maybe we can fuck some English girls." said Alexis.

"I fucking love British chicks. I'd probably want to do that," replied John as he removed the last label from the last DVD. "That's it. We're done. What time you picking me up?"

"Four in the morning. Everything else is already in my trunk. I'll just need to gas up before we get on the turnpike," replied Alexis.

John stood up and proceeded to exit the room. Just as he opened the door, Leo arrived at the top of the stairs. He, too, was drunk and high and likely on some other drugs. John immediately knew that Leo's presence would delay his exit from the house. Twenty minutes later, he found himself in the back of Leo's truck smoking a blunt with the Garcia brothers. The entire cabin was fogged out, and everybody was high beyond measure.

"So, what are you two little shits doing tomorrow?" asked Leo.

"Gettin' paid, motha-fucka... we're going to rent a space at the Swap Shop and set up a table and sell everything for cheap. There's something for everyone at the Ganked Depot!" said Alexis like a cheap, used-car salesman from the television commercials.

"That's what you're calling it? Ganked-Depot? It's got a nice ring," replied Leo before taking a hit of the blunt. "People might want to buy things from you, but I don't think anyone will want to give their money to this white mother-fucker right here," said Leo as he pointed at quiet John.

"Hey, hey, hey, there's no need for racist talk. Why you always gotta shit on the white man?" replied John. Playful racism was a huge part of the inside humor that he shared with Leo.

"Cause you a honkie-ass mother-fucka who still owes me for that eighth I sold you. Now you over here smoking my shit again: replied Leo in a comedic, urban tone.

"I think we're going to make a lot of money, bro," said Alexis to his brother.

"You guys are fucking crazy for doing this. After all the times Mom and Dad took us to that place, I never thought you, of all people, would be selling shit there one day. Just don't get caught. Dad would be pissed he had to bail you out," advised Leo.

"Oh, no, we don't want to upset papa," said John to engage Leo.

He got exactly what he asked for. Leo quickly turned around and started digging his rock-hard fist into John's ribs. John could always count on Leo for a good laugh. It was all silly talk, nothing that was to be taken seriously.

John was close to the Garcia family. Despite being so different from a cultural perspective, he appreciated the family's cohesiveness. Nights like those, getting stoned and drunk at the house with no girls in sight, were all too common during that period of their lives. But the camaraderie made those boring nights something special. They smoked a few more bowls of Leo's weed before John finally left home.

The excitement of the day was enough to get Alexis and John out of their beds despite still being drunk. Alexis arrived at John's apartment at four a.m. and found him standing outside, smoking a cigarette.

"Hey, buddy! Feel like making some money today!?" said an overexcited Alexis, who noticed his friend's exhausted face. John stepped inside the car while Alexis continued to stare at him with the face of a deranged psycho. "Let's do this," was all John said.

They drove to a gas station that was just off the turnpike to get gas and buy beer. After filling the tank, Alexis walked inside the store and acknowledged the clerk standing behind the register. He walked to the beer section to weigh his beverage options. Because it would be a long day, he figured they needed at least an eighteen-pack. Therefore, he chose a box of Miller Lite and proceeded to pay for it.

"Can I please have a pack of Marlboro Lights?" he said to the clerk.

"Starting the party early, I seer said the good-humored store clerk.

Alexis smiled at the comment before grabbing his items and leaving. He walked out the door and noticed that John was not in the car.

"Where is that drunk bastard?" he thought.

The drunk bastard had a bright idea while waiting for Alexis. He noticed a big American flag hanging from the gas station sign and decided that he wanted it for their display. Without any regression, John got out of the car, walked to the flag, and took it off the clips.

"What the fuck are you doing?" said Alexis as John casually approached the car with a flag under his arm.

"I got us a flag," replied John before getting into the car. The clerk noticed and ran from his register to confront the boys. As Alexis was putting the key in the ignition, the clerk started banging repeatedly on his window while yelling profanities. It startled the boys. But they just laughed from the excitement and drove away, throwing the clerk to the ground in the process.

"What the hell did you do that for?" asked Alexis.

"Hey, man. Just trust me. This flag is going to draw a lot of attention," said John as they drove onto the Florida turnpike.

It was 4:45 a.m. and still dark when they arrived at the flea market in Sunrise, Florida. The fifteen-acre property held one of the largest flea markets in the world and a multiscreen drive-in theatre in the evenings. Alexis and John were among the earliest vendors to arrive that day, but more were arriving by the minute.

"Do we have to register?" asked John, who was slowly awakening.

"Yeah, I'm just following that car in front to see where he goes," replied Alexis as they drove under the giant movie screens using the high beams.

There were workers guiding the vendors onto the premise. A Haitian man with a baseball cap eventually approached Alexis's car and said, "Space three-thirty-three, just follow the van."

Alexis followed the van and parked his car behind it at space 333. Then they stepped out of the car, stretched their legs, and proceeded to the registration booth. There were multiple vendors setting up for the day. Some people were already in the process of assembling their canopies next to their cars. The abundance of old, rusty trucks and aged sedans indicated to Alexis that they were among poor individuals doing their best to survive.

Alexis paid the man at the booth thirty dollars for the space, one table, and the canopy set. The poles for the canopy set were attached to cement blocks, so they had to use a cart to wheel the items back to their space.

"This is it, Thibault. There's no going back," said Alexis as he pushed off the ground to ride the cart like a kid in the grocery store.

"I can't fucking believe we're finally here. This is great, Guapos," replied John, who was enjoying a cigarette while walking next to the cart.

They arrived at the space and unloaded the poles and the canopy. John was not as thrilled as Alexis to build their booth. He just reverted to his dreary persona and finished another cigarette while Alexis worked. Alexis spread out the canopy tarp, aligned the poles at each corner, and tied the canopy to each pole.

"That's that," said Alexis. He noticed that the table was still on the floor and that John had not done anything to help.

"Are you going to fucking help?" asked Alexis.

"Man, what did I tell you? I'm thinking, okay? I got something big on my mind," replied John.

"Got what?" replied Alexis, who was humored by John's cryptic messages.

"I think we should pull in the Grand-Am sideways to block off any potential thieves. That way, we only have to monitor one side," suggested John.

"I like that idea. Here are the keys," said Alexis.

"And we can just smoke and drink inside the car without anybody else seeing us," added John to further sell his contribution.

"Oh, that reminds me. My brother gave me a couple of methadone to make the day go a little easier," said Alexis.

"Whoa, that's some strong shit. Isn't that what they give heroin addicts?" asked John.

"Yeah, that's what he said," replied Alexis.

John reversed the car onto the west side of the rectangular space. He stepped out of the car with the American flag he stole from the gas station, cut pieces of scotch tape from a roll that Alexis brought, and hung the flag over the display table. He then stepped back and observed the display. But as appealing as it looked, he felt that something was missing.

"Hey, did you make any posters?" he asked Alexis.

"Yes, I did. They're in the trunk. I made two."

John grabbed the posters from the trunk and proceeded to hang one on each side of the flag.

One poster read: "NEW! UNUSED! CDs AND DVDs!" The other poster read: "CDs FOR $8.00 / DVDs FOR $10.00."

John took another step back and confirmed he was content with the display. He lit another cigarette just as the sun was starting to touch the evening sky. After taking his first drag and returning the pack to his pocket, he took a moment to observe the rest of their surroundings.

"This is fucking great. I can't believe we pulled it off," repeated John.

"Yeah, and I think we're going to sell a lot of shit. That circus and food court bring in a lot of people on Sundays," said Alexis as he placed the perfectly arranged DVD boxes on the table. There were fifty brand-new DVDs in each of the four boxes.

Next, they unloaded the boxes of CDs and arranged the small signs that indicated the music genres. Finally, John opened two folding chairs behind the table and put the cooler in the middle.

"And now, my friend, we just wait," said Alexis.

"Fuck that. Let's start drinking. We've been working too hard," said John as he opened the cooler. "Whoa, shit. You got liquor, too?" he added after finding a bottle of rum.

"Yeah, there's rum and coke in there. I even got limes," replied Alexis.

"What about food?" asked John.

"I got two Publix subs, mac and cheese, chips, Colombian chicharrones, and a key lime pie," said Alexis, who was trying to relax in his chair before the morning crowd arrived.

John opened the bottle of rum and poured it into a plastic cup. He added the coke and threw in some cubes of ice before handing it to Alexis.

"Here you go, Guapos," he said.

"Whoa, shit. I didn't tell you. I also got us a couple of bars. This day is going to be great!" said Alexis in a juvenile undertone with a big smile on his face. He reached into his pocket and pulled out two Xanax bars, giving one to John and keeping the other for himself.

"Well, my friend, cheers to the moment," said Alexis as he held his drink in the air.

"Cheers, Guapos," said John in a terrible Mexican accent.

They hit cups and washed down the Xanax bars with their first chug. It wasn't even six-thirty in the morning. At only eighteen years old, they felt invincible and capable of conquering the day. Whatever consequences were waiting for them, they felt proud knowing that it would be their burden to bear; not their mother's, not their father's, not anyone's. They felt as free and independent as they had ever felt in their young lives.

The first customers started to arrive around 7:30 a.m. Those were the dedicated wanderers of the flea market, the regulars, always hoping to be the first to spot a hidden treasure. One after the other, people gradually breezed through the fenced walkway. Alexis and John, already inebriated, were in the process of devouring their breakfast sandwiches when a customer approached the booth. It was a middle-aged man with a Guy Harvey shirt and cargo shorts, holding a cup of coffee and wearing shades.

"How you doin', boys? I actually came here today to find an album. It's the new Radiohead. Do you have that?" asked the man in a thick New York accent.

"Yes, we do! It's right here," said John before grabbing the CD from one of the boxes.

"Wow! What else do you have?" asked the man.

"Look around. These are all new… unopened. We have DVDs as well. There's reggae, rock, classic rock, classical, jazz, pop, whatever you like," said Alexis, who'd gotten up from his chair to close the sale.

"This is a great collection. Where did you guys get all these?" asked the nosey stranger. He was asking way more questions than either John or Alexis wanted to hear. When he did not hear a response, the man looked up at the young, stone-faced vendors and decided to quit the small talk.

"Eh, it doesn't matter. I'll give you fifty bucks for these five CDs and these two DVDs. What do you say?"

"I'd say, no. The price for CDs is eight, and for DVDs, it's ten. These are all new and unused. The best I can do is sixty," replied Alexis in a stern tone. He did not want to get taken advantage of due to his young age. That is why he was prepared to negotiate.

The man took a moment to think. He knew he had some type of leverage in the deal, but the boys did not look too desperate. Everyone there knew that more people would arrive throughout the day to buy the items. So, the customer swallowed his pride and eyeballed Alexis and John before saying, "You got yourself a deal."

It was not even eight in the morning, and they had already made a sale. Alexis held the money in his pocket while John went to the car to celebrate. He took a few hits of weed and rolled down the windows to release the smoke. John did not care about who could smell it. There was only one adjacent vendor and a few other vendors without canopies on the south side of the lot. Most were of Caribbean descent, mostly people from Haiti, the Bahamas, or Jamaica. Almost none had anything of value to sell, only used and hoarded items that were scattered on a tarp.

The next customer arrived five minutes later, but he did not come from the parking lot. He was a vendor from the other side of the flea market. He looked to be of Indian descent, but that was just Alexis's educated guess.

"Do you have used DVDs?" asked the young Hindi man in traditional clothing.

"No, sorry, everything here is new. We even got that new Jackie Chan movie. Do you like him? He's funny," said Alexis to the man like a bold, wise-ass youth.

He continued to search the items with diligence. He paid the most attention to the films, thoroughly going through each one and reading the summaries and reviews on the case. To Alexis, he was seemingly reviewing their inventory with no interest in buying anything. With every passing minute, he became more annoyed by his behavior. Still, despite being intoxicated, he opted not to get confrontational. He just sat in his chair and sipped his drink while trying to ignore the man.

John stepped out of the car, releasing a thick cloud of smoke into the air. By that time, a young couple had arrived at the booth in search of a good deal.

"Whoa, shit, where did all these people come from?" asked John.

"These guys just got here... and this dude does not buy anything. I think he's another vendor scoping out the competition," said Alexis.

John did not appreciate hearing that. He was less patient when drunk. While wearing his shades, he rubbed his hands on his face and chugged the last of his drink. With a little aggression, he placed the cup on the table and approached the man with an agenda.

"Excuse me, sir. Is there anything I can help you with?" he asked.

The man didn't respond. He just mumbled a sound with his mouth, never looking up at the little punk behind the table. Again, that was something that John did not appreciate. He found his behavior to be disrespectful.

"Sir are you looking to buy anything?" politely asked John. But still, there was no response. The man just kept looking at the movies.

Maybe it was the combination of alcohol and Xanax bars, or maybe it was his pent-up aggression, but John felt a sudden surge of confidence. He just stared at the man who was noting their inventory until it became unbearable to tolerate.

"Get the fuck away from here if you're not going to buy anything! We don't want you to come back! Do you hear me! We don't want you to come back!" said John boldly.

The man stood tall and held his arms out as though saying, as though claiming his innocence. But he also looked angry, like he was ready to fight.

"Don't fucking come back, man!" added Alexis.

"Hey, ya, faka-yoo!" said the man while walking away and

flipping Alexis the middle finger.

The young couple was alarmed by the confrontation, but they continued to look through the outstanding music selection. She chose a few pop albums and two Jennifer Lopez films. He chose two hardcore albums and a U2 box set. Alexis and John made one-hundred dollars on the sale.

The rest of the morning brought consistent business, more than the boys ever anticipated. Their fun adventure quickly became a full day of work. As the sun was making the morning hot, the entire flea market became overrun with customers. There were people of all ages, races, and religious backgrounds gathering at the market for a day of shopping and entertainment.

It was highly likely that many vendors were thieves like John and Alexis. Some people sold car stereos, other people sold car rims, and many dedicated themselves to cheap electronics. But those items were not as liquid as brand-new CDs and DVDs. That was why John and Alexis were getting a lot of attention.

Throughout the course of the morning, the boys took turns manning the station and going inside the car for a smoke break. They made drinks in the open where customers could see, showing no regard or shame.

"Hey, Guapos!" said John during the morning rush.

"Yo," replied Alexis.

"I think we should take those methadone," suggested John.

"Do you really think we need them?" asked Alexis, who was also trying to watch the people looking through the inventory.

"Absolutely! It's a beautiful fucking day, and we're making

money. I'm drunk. I'm high. I'm on pills. But something's missing," replied John while stepping towards his friend and grinning with depravity. Alexis knew that nothing would stop John from taking the methadone at that moment.

He walked to the car, grabbed his book bag, and pulled two 40-milligram pills from the back pocket. He noticed that each pill had the number 54|142 written on them. Neither had ever tried a methadone, but they were experienced enough with drugs to hopefully maintain standard functionality.

"It's kind of a big pill. Do we take it all?" asked John while staring at the massive opiate.

"I don't think so. Let's split a quarter each and see how we feel," said Alexis while staring at the pill. "We can even sprinkle a little on a blunt and smoke that," he added to John's delight.

Before anyone could notice, they washed down a ten-milligram quarter with rum and coke. After that, John proceeded to attend to the customers while Alexis went in the car to roll a blunt with sprinkled methadone. By that point, the boys were feeling invincible.

The effect of the pill kicked in quickly. But that did not stop Alexis from smoking nearly half the blunt before deciding to go back to work. The car was fogged beyond measure, and again, as a result, an immense cloud of smoke shot into the air as the door opened. Some of the customers noticed, but the cheap inventory kept their interest.

At one point, they were too inebriated to properly attend a group of brothers who were trapeze performers in the circus. They were wearing casual shorts and footwear but still had their trapeze shirts on.

Both degenerates were sunk into their chairs, wearing their shades and barely moving. Alexis felt as though he was having an out-of-body experience. He could hear everything the trapeze brothers were saying, but all he could do was smile and say 'alright' to whatever they were mumbling. His vision was nothing more than a shivering pane of human figures.

John was the same. He was barely able to get out of his chair to make the transaction. One of the trapeze brothers handed him money, and John fell back into his chair while saying, "Sorry, no bags."

The young man just left the money and took the items. Alexis turned to his best friend and slurred, "Life is beautiful and frightening at the same time. Thank God for drugs and alcohol."

Chapter Four

They made more than two-thousand dollars in profit that morning. The customers continued to arrive in full force. The booth also drew a lot of attention from the other vendors whose sales numbers could not compare. It was not easy for them to see two punks make so much money in a handful of hours.

"Damn, bro, I didn't think it would be this much work," said John after handing a customer change for a purchase.

"Do you want to take a break?" asked Alexis.

"Yeah, I'll go for a walk and check this place out. One of the trapeze boys said the show starts at two."

"Alright, the main vendors are under that big canopy. The food court and the circus and arcade are all inside the building," advised Alexis.

John stepped away from the booth to explore the venue. He came from a prominent family in Boynton Beach. That is where he was born and raised. It was not the most diverse upbringing, and he was not used to being in places where there were so many people of color. John was not ignorant of the world or intimidated by anyone, but his friendship with Alexis had broadened his international horizons over the years.

The white boy casually strolled among the Hindi, the Haitians, the Jamaicans, the Asians, and the Hispanics, observing their businesses, products, and distinctive negotiation styles. As soon as he approached the east side of the main building, euphoric John ran into four massive elephants. They were standing in enclosures under the custom-built elephant holding area, wearing their demeaning circus costumes and looking ragged.

The view was alarming. After swaying while staring at the giant creatures, he slowly stepped forward to regain his gait. John was bothered by the wooden boundaries that left them hardly any room to move. There was only enough room for them to walk to the mountainous pile of hay that was thrown against the building wall.

While staring at the ghastly sight, he swayed off balance again and bumped into a boy who was walking with his friends toward the building entrance. They were all carrying sports posters, magazines, and other memorabilia. And they were all in a rush to get inside the building.

"Sorry, kid," John muttered.

He was intrigued to see where they were going. The smiles on their faces and the glimmer in their eyes was a look he remembered having as a kid, back when times were simpler and his family was together.

John followed the boys into the main building and immediately felt as though he had stepped onto another planet. There were bizarre, loud sounds coming at him from all angles, making the place seem like some type of funhouse or an alien spaceship.

Most of the sounds came from the massive arcade where all the classic video games were on display. In a time when arcades were slowly becoming a thing of the past, that flea market kept it as a staple of its overall operation. John was impressed.

He entered the cafeteria, which spanned the entire first floor. From where he stood, swaying from left to right because of the drugs and alcohol in his system, John could see a multitude of diverse places to eat with loud electric signs. This included mid-eastern food, Asian food, Greek food, Latin food, pizza places, and American barbecue. To John, the Swap Shop proved to be as intriguing as Alexis made it out to be.

His eyes then drifted to the middle of the building where the circus ring was located. John stared at every colorful detail in a delayed moment of time. He could not believe that an actual circus was taking place at a flea market. It was a bizarre, trippy, and overwhelming scene all at once. There was a ringmaster, clowns, death-defying performances, and all the other elements of a live circus.

As the trapeze brothers performed their act, John moseyed through the crowd of families, ignoring the show while trying to find where the children with the memorabilia went. He noticed a crowd at the far end of the cafeteria, next to the pizzeria, and proceeded to investigate.

There were children, teenagers, and adults gathered for what seemed to be a baseball card convention. John was welcomed by a huge billboard with a picture of the owner of the sports museum. The man from the television commercials. His name was Herb Bowman. He was one of the main sponsors of the event.

John started browsing through the display cases to gauge the quality of the items. It was not long before he caught the attention of a vendor.

"How are you, young man?" said an old man with long hair who was wearing an old rock concert shirt from the seventies. He looked like he had not showered in days.

"How much is this Mark McGwire rookie-set worth?" asked

John without ever looking the man in the eye.

"That set goes for $125 dollars. It includes a signed program from the game when he broke Roger Maris's record," replied the vendor.

John knew it was a fair price, but it was more than he could afford. He declined the offer and walked away from the booth to see what else was on display. He eventually arrived at the grand area that was reserved for Mr. Herb Bowman. He was the distinguished owner of the Sports Museum and Collectibles in Boca Raton. He was the top dog among the other collectors and was not ashamed to boast about it. He always held a smug look on his face and did nothing to correct his lisp, which continually ejected saliva into the air.

At first, John observed Herb from a distance as he arrogantly bickered with a group of men over the price of one of his items. After the unconvinced shoppers left, Herb Bowman returned to polishing his most prized possession, a two-million-dollar Honus Wagner baseball card. It was displayed in a case that was both fireproof and bulletproof. Because it drew so much attention at the show, Herb stood nearby it to discuss the card's history with whoever would listen.

"The card was made by the American Tobacco Company in 1909. But Wagner halted their production because he did not want kids to smoke. Since so few were made, it became the most expensive card in the world in the thirties. You want to know how much it went for back then?" asked Herb to an uneducated, middle-aged customer.

"Can't be much," replied one customer.

"It was originally valued at fifty dollars. And at the time, it was the most expensive card in the world," said Herb, with mounds of fluid spewing from his mouth.

John fell into a trance after laying his eyes on the card. Everything around him went silent as his mind processed all the rising emotions. He slowly approached Herb's booth, keeping his head down while looking at the card. Because the item was so rare and expensive, Herb had to hire large security guards for added protection.

Unfortunately for John, his faded Marlins baseball hat nearly covered his eyes and made him look suspicious, drawing the attention of Herb's security.

John admired the thick, protective case as two guards watched him from a distance. He noticed that it was much smaller than contemporary baseball cards and relatively worn out due to its age. But the card was still considered to be in near-mint condition.

"See anything that piques your interest?" asked Herb.

John was in no condition to converse with the man. But he knew he had to say something to get more time to view the card.

"You have a lot of good stuff over there. Why is this card so... protected? What makes it any different?" asked John to blend in with the crowd.

"Heh! You can't be serious, boy! This is Honus Wagner, the most expensive baseball card to ever exist!" rudely replied Herb while chuckling.

"That would explain the fancy case. But if that card belonged to me, I would never put it on display. You never know who's watching," said John, unconsciously thinking out loud.

The comment put Herb on alert. He was cynical, always on the lookout for people trying to plot against him. He also felt it was awkward that somebody attending a baseball collectibles show had no clue who Honus Wagner was.

"Well, I don't think that'll be an issue here. You see those two security guards? Well, they're strapped pretty well and will shoot anyone I tell them to. Now, if you're done looking around, I need to get back to business," said Herb.

John took one last look at the display case to memorize its details. He wanted every inch, every corner, and every lock embedded in his memory. After that, he browsed through a few more booths. He ended up buying the Topps Refractor Gold— Johann Santana rookie card before walking away from the small convention with a new sense of purpose.

Back at the booth, Alexis was calmly handling the afternoon rush of customers while also eyeballing a group of shady punks who kept lingering around the space. It appeared he had been targeted.

"Thank you for your purchase. Enjoy the movies," said Alexis to a female customer without taking his eyes off the potential vandals.

Just then, one of the young prowlers, a hood rat, bounced her way to the table. The little Latina, with too much makeup on her face, attempted to distract Alexis with her over-developed features. She made every attempt to look sexy and keep his attention, twirling her hair and licking a sucker while browsing the music. At the same time, the three other punks gathered at different ends of the space, making it harder for Alexis to monitor them at the same time.

The teen vixen bent over the table and let her breasts hang in front of Alexis' face. Her small tang-top barely covered anything, and Alexis couldn't look away.

When the punks noticed the distraction working, they executed their scheme.

The one on the left grabbed two handfuls of DVDs and started running, dropping a bunch on the ground. Alexis noticed what was happening and turned around to see the other two punks. The one that was lingering by the back of the space attempted to grab a box of CDs that was on the floor. The weakling struggled to gain momentum while holding the box, so Alexis ran around the table and drop-kicked him on his back. After the punk dropped the box, he stood up and ran away. The third punk froze after seeing his friend's failed attempt, and Alexis also chased him away.

Two hundred feet to the west, the first punk thought he had gotten away with the loot. But John was walking in his direction and saw Alexis chase down the third punk. He thought quickly and stuck his foot outward, tripping punk number one onto the concrete. The DVDs scattered everywhere, and the troubled youth opted to stand up and keep running. John chuckled, not really knowing what'd happened, and calmly picked up the items. Then he looked at Alexis, who was huffing and puffing by the table.

"Dude, what the fuck happened?" asked John.

"Three little fuckers just tried to rob us. I kicked one down, and the other ran away. I don't think they got away with anything," said an excited Alexis. "Where the fuck were you?"

"Guapos," said John before putting his hand on his buddy's shoulder. "We need to sit down, smoke a joint, and talk about something really important."

"What the fuck are you talking about?" asked Alexis with skepticism while reorganizing the inventory. "I'm not in the mood to hear you babble. We've got money to make."

Despite Alexis's resistance, they sat down on the lawn chairs and sparked a fresh joint. It was necessary for Alexis to smoke and calm his nerves after almost being robbed. His adrenaline was still pumping.

"I should've stomped on that dude's head when I had the chance," he said before taking a hit of the joint.

"Hey, forget about that. We have more important things to discuss," said John.

"Like what? We should be working. Go stand out front and bring people in so we can sell all this shit," said Alexis while expelling a cloud of smoke.

"Forget about that. It's beans compared to what I have in mind," said John before taking an extended hit. "Do you know who Honus Wagner is?"

"Motherfucker, I was shortstop on our championship team. Of course, I know who Honus Wagner is. What about him?" replied Alexis.

"Do you know that his card is worth two-million dollars?" asked John.

"I didn't know it was worth that much. But it's that little stamp card. I have a few replicas in my old collection," said Alexis.

"Exactly, you had those too. Well, that same card, except the real one, is worth two-million dollars," said John.

"Okay, so why do I give a fuck?" replied Alexis.

"Because that card is at the Sports Museum in Boca, and I want to steal it," revealed John.

"What the fuck do you mean? How fucked up are you?" said Alexis.

"I'm pretty fucked up, but this is something I've been thinking about for a while. The card is in that building right now. The owner brought it for a baseball card show. I saw it. It's a fucking thing of beauty," expressed John.

"What the hell do you want to do? Steal it from the show?" asked Alexis.

"No, of course not," said John before taking another hit. "I want to break into the museum and take it. But I need you to help me think of a way to pull it off," replied John.

He gave his friend a moment to observe the idea. Alexis did not overreact negatively in the way that John anticipated. Instead, the idea calmed Alexis. The Swap Shop heist made him feel invincible. So, he was open to listening more about John's idea. They spent the rest of the day making money and brainstorming ideas for John's proposition.

The sun was setting when John and Alexis decided to close the shop. They were one of the last vendors there because the customers did not stop arriving. But in the end, they had to stop drinking, smoking weed, and taking pills. It was time for the boys to go home. Before leaving, John sold the remaining inventory to

another vendor for dirt cheap. When it was all said and done, the
boys made over three thousand dollars that day.

47

Chapter Five

It was the fall of 1996 when John and Alexis played on a championship little league team. That year, the West Boynton Tigers were projected to win the state title for a second time. They posed with determination for the team photos that were taken before the first game of the playoffs. In the center of that team picture were the star players, John Thibault and Alexis Garcia. They were an impenetrable tandem that led the team to an undefeated season.

"Okay, boys! I want you to look like champions. We have a playoff game to win today," said a young Luke Thibault.

The team responded to their coach like loyal soldiers, "Yes, sir!"

"That's right! That's what I want to see. Perfection! Domination!" added Coach Luke.

He continued to pump up his team as they stood in line to take individual pictures. Each player took three pictures: one in the crouching position, one in the batting position, and a third picture in the throwing position. As the players and the photographers became distracted in the process, Coach Luke calmly took sips of his coffee, which was mixed with bourbon.

After the pictures were finished, the team moved to the batting cages to take turns warming up and stretching. By that time, Coach Luke was drunk. He leaned against the batting cage and repeated the same tips to the batter.

"Watch your form!" or "Follow through!" and "Eye on the ball!"

John and Alexis were tossing grounders to one another when they noticed the coach's condition. They knew he'd been drinking all day and feared the possibility of him making a scene.

"Hey, Johnny! Get over here and hit a few! Why you boys hiding over there like a couple of queers?" said Luke to John.

Young John and young Alexis cautiously walked to the cage for their turn at batting. They knew the coach was belligerent once the homophobic insults started. There was no way to predict what he would say or do next.

Alexis was the first to step inside the cage. He had five home runs that season and was hoping for a sixth that day. After getting into his batting stance, he gave the ball machine a piercing stare in anticipation of the pitch. The ball ejected towards him at eighty-five miles per hour, and he hit it with conviction. His power echoed deep into the atmosphere before getting back into batting stance.

"Damn, Alexis! What's in them frijoles?" said Coach Luke.

Alexis hated those types of comments. But in the white-dominated city of Boynton, they were common. From an early age, he realized he could not fight every time someone said something racist. So, unless such a comment came from a stranger, he was usually passive about it.

As John was warming up with the bat, Luke decided to give him some words of advice. He chugged the remainder of the coffee-bourbon mix, tossed away the cup, and approached his son. John was terrified about what was coming next.

"I gotta get some more coffee. But I wanted to tell you that you're dropping your shoulder when you swing. It's throwing you completely off balance. I don't want to see that shit today. Do you hear me?" mumbled an aggressive Luke.

"Just go get your coffee and let me hit," said a disappointed John.

"Hey! I'm your father! You listen to your father!" replied Luke. "If I see you drop that shoulder, I'll fucking kill you. Do you understand?"

Alexis heard the tone and stopped hitting the balls. He was never scared of Luke. And he never hesitated to intervene whenever John was being attacked.

"John! It's your turn," said Alexis.

John walked away from his father and entered the cage armed with anger. He choked up on the bat with an extra-tight grip and let the rage overcome his swing. He hit each ball harder than the previous, striking fear into the opponents who watched. Meanwhile, Luke walked away with the team's assistant coach to grab a coffee at the food stand.

It wasn't the first time the Tigers had to play with a drunk coach. Despite his problem, Luke was an intelligent and effective coach who always had his players ready to play their best. The first-round game was against the Vipers, who came with a sub-par record but had the best player in the league. His name was Brian Stitt, and he was the biggest twelve-year-old in all of Palm Beach County. He played pitcher and was known for throwing fastballs over ninety miles per hour.

The Tigers started the game strong against Stitt. John was the lead-off hitter and drilled a hit into left field for an early double. The second hitter, Cody Williams, centerfielder, tapped a bunt toward third and managed to get on first base. Hitter number three was the third baseman, Andy Lambert. The Brooklyn native hit his twenty-first R.B.I. of the season to bring John home.

Alexis was the fourth batter. He was calm and loose when he walked up to the plate. He had earned a reputation as a strong hitter, making the outfielders play farther out than usual. As was his ritual, he used the bat to hit the dirt off his cleats before getting into his hitting stance. He stared directly at the pitcher as an intimidation factor.

While staring at Alexis, Brian mouthed the words, "fuck this guy." Then he got in his pitching stance, turned to the side with legs spread apart, and held the ball in glove against his torso. Without warning, Brian fired a high fastball that got Alexis to swing and miss.

"Strike one!" yelled the umpire.

"What the hell are you swinging for!?" yelled Luke. "Calm down and find your shot!"

The catcher threw the ball back to the pitcher, who had a cocky smirk on his face. Alexis had to step away from the plate to stretch his neck from side to side. Then he returned to the plate, choked up on the bat, and took his stance again. Brian Stitt received the signal from the catcher, returned to his pitching stance, and fired a sinker that almost got Alexis to swing.

"Ball!" yelled the umpire.

After getting back in his stance, Alexis noticed Brian Stitt consecutively nodding his head 'no' in response to the catcher's pitch signals. That told Alexis that he had the pitcher's attention. From there, he would simply wait for the perfect moment to swing hard.

When they finally agreed on a pitch, Alexis loosened his grip on the bat. Without time to think, Brian delivered a heater to the bottom right corner of the strike zone. He let his ego take control and challenged Alexis head-on. It turned out to be a gamble that did not pay off for the lethal pitcher.

Alexis launched a home run into left field, putting the Tigers ahead by four runs in the first inning. The ball cleared the fence by almost one hundred feet, giving fans and parents much to cheer for. Alexis rounded the bases and arrived at home plate, where his teammates were waiting to congratulate him.

Brian Stitt retaliated the next inning with a two-run homer of his own. After that, the fifth batter hit a line drive over John's head for a double. John knew the error infuriated his dad and avoided eye-contacted with him after the play ended. But as the next batter walked to the plate, he could feel Luke's piercing stare from the dugout.

The Tigers finished the first inning with a four- two lead over the Vipers. From the second inning forward, the pitchers took control of the game. The Tigers maintained a raucous dugout to stay pumped, cheering for their teammates and against the opponent with vigor. Despite the competitive nature of the game, they were kids living in the moment.

John did his best to match the team's excitement, but he kept looking at his dad every time he took a drink from his cup. At that point, John knew that something was imminent… that some type of disastrous scene would soon unfold. After six innings, Luke was barely able to construct and deliver verbal communication. He just stood with his shades on and stared at the lineup on his clipboard.

It was the bottom of the eighth inning, and the score had not changed. Both teams battled to take the lead, but the pitchers and fielding defense dominated the game. John stepped to the plate for his fourth time at bat. He had a man in scoring position on third base, and the team had two outs. By that point, Luke was sitting on the bench in a blank state of mind, trying his best to maintain an unalarming posture.

John refrained from swinging at the first pitch. The umpire called, "ball!" Brian Stitt was still pitching, but John felt he had nothing left.

The determined pitcher took off his cap to wipe the sweat from his face. After taking a few deep breaths, he returned to his pitching stance. He threw a curve ball that landed outside the strike zone, giving John a two-ball advantage. Luke then stood from the bench to observe the next pitch. But it was hardly to encourage his son. Instead, his mind could only see the error and construct belligerent criticism.

After hearing his father clear the phlegm in his throat, John knew that the monster had emerged. He could feel him through his peripheral senses. But instead of turning around to acknowledge him, John returned to the plate and gripped his bat with both hands. Brian Stitt agreed on signals with the pitcher, stood in position, and fired a curve ball. John targeted the ball, swung, and missed.

"Strike!" yelled the umpire.

Up until that point, John was four-for-four, having gotten on base each time that day. But for some reason, Luke's mind could only focus on his form.

"Time!" yelled Luke. "Johnny, come here!"

John wouldn't disobey his father, not in front of such a large crowd. He turned around and approached his father on guard.

"What is it, Dad?" he said.

"You keep fucking dropping your shoulder. How many times did I tell you not to do that?"

"I'm not dropping my shoulder. My swing is fine. Can you just let me hit!?" replied John.

That was when Alexis decided to intervene. He walked out of the dugout and got in between father and son. He was calm and did nothing to worsen the situation. But there was nothing he could do to control Luke's anger.

"What the fuck did you say? Do you think I give two fucks that we're out here? Huh? Don't ever fucking disrespect me in public," snarled Luke in John's face.

"You're fucking insane. I'm going to hit," said John as he turned away.

Luke grabbed his son's arm with all his strength. John turned around and accidentally swung the bat at his dad's face. That was when Luke pushed Alexis down and charged at his son like a rhino. He grabbed John by the neck with his left hand and punched his face twice with his right fist. John took the punches like a heavyweight champion and stayed on his feet. His mother and little brother had witnessed everything from the bleachers. She yelled frantically for her husband to stop.

"Luke! Get the fuck off him!" she yelled.

The umpire quickly intervened, preventing Luke from killing John. As a result, Luke aimed his rage at the umpire and knocked him out with a right cross. After that, the other adults intervened and restrained Luke. The police eventually arrived, and the game was canceled for a later date. Luke was arrested, and the umpire up would go on to press charges.

That was the traumatizing moment that defined the rest of John's life. The rage and humility that he experienced that day would never leave far from his mind. His parents separated soon after, officially divorcing three years later. Along the way, Luke was permanently kicked out of the family business for misusing funds and cutting all communications with his father and brothers. He developed a cocaine habit, and his financial situation pushed him to the brink of suicide.

As for John, he became a pothead and only played baseball for one more season. He and Alexis only became interested in three things after that: girls, punk-rock music, and partying. They drank and smoked their way through catholic high school until Alexis was eventually expelled for fighting. John transferred to a public school at the end of his junior year because his parents divorced and stopped paying tuition. Although they went to different schools after that, the two degenerates remained close friends.

Through it all, John did his best to appreciate the little beauty that life had to offer. But his family's demise became a burden that only he was willing to carry, and his outlook on life became numb and void.

Chapter Six

On a night like any other, John closed the music section and walked to the bathroom to inspect if any items had been left there. He removed a magazine next to the sink and then proceeded to check the stalls. But when he tried opening the handicap stall, he found that it was locked. And after shaking the door a few times, he heard a woman's voice.

"I... I can't hold it. I'm slipping...," she whispered.

John knew the sound of sex when he heard it. He played dumb and walked away to pretend he was leaving. He even opened the door to make it seem like he had left the bathroom. After waiting a few seconds, he heard the couple continue their intercourse. Inside the stall, a woman was sitting on top of her partner with her arms and legs spread in the air.

"Just close your legs a little, babe," said the large woman as she adjusted her position.

"Alright, just let me pop you up," said the larger boyfriend as he cooperated.

"There, that's better," said the woman to confirm that his penis was well inserted.

They continued to slap skins on the porcelain toilet. Her hands pressed hard against the stall, shaking its walls and almost detaching the hinges. The sex was sloppy and intense, but John wasn't going to let it end with an orgasm.

With all his strength, he kicked the stall door open. He was welcomed by the sight of two naked pigs and their genitals. But he kept his composure and didn't make a scene.

"This is disgusting. Put on your clothes and never come back," he said to the frozen couple.

"Sure, pal... we'll be out of here in a second," said the man, who was wearing only a baseball cap. The woman popped off him, they got dressed, and walked out of the bathroom. John returned to the music section when he was stopped by Tanisha, who was giving the new hire a tour of the store.

"John, I'm glad I ran into you. This is Shannon. She'll be joining us for the holidays," said Tanisha. "Shannon, this is John. He works in the music section." The strangers shook hands, both sensing an instant physical attraction.

"Are you from Boynton?" asked John with confidence.

"Actually, no. I've been in Florida for three months. I moved from New Jersey," replied Shannon.

"That's where my family is from, but I've been here all my life," said John.

John and Shannon projected smiles to each other. There was a pleasant moment of silence that followed, with Tanisha standing awkwardly in the middle.

"Well, Shannon, there's still a lot more to see," said Tanisha in her peppiest tone.

"It was nice to meet you," said John.

"It was nice to meet you, too," replied Shannon.

Tanisha and Shannon walked away to see the rest of the store. John returned to the music section and found Angelica going through the new-release albums stored behind the counter.

"You didn't tell me there was a new 'Disturbed' album. Or are we just getting it like three months late?" she said.

"I'm not sure about that one. I think it's new," replied John, who was still thinking of his encounter with Shannon. He wanted to be alone and walked away from the register to avoid Angelica.

"Ugh!" expressed Angelica in a disappointed but light-hearted tone. "How disrespectful. Don't walk away from me, Mr. Thibault!" John used to think her childish expressions were cute. But as of late, he found it annoying and unbearable.

"So... am I still sleeping over tonight?" she said while chasing him.

"Um, yeah, I guess. I mean, I'm tired. I might just pass out," replied John.

"You're breaking your promise to me. Ugh, I feel rejected," said the Wiccan.

"Who is the librarian with Lori? I saw you two talking," asked a jealous Angelica.

"Some girl she hired," replied John while reorganizing the CDs in the listening section.

"Well, she looks boring. So, I guess I'll call you later to see if you're awake," said Angelica as she walked away.

"I'm leaving once I'm done cleaning up. Come over in an hour," said John to entertain her idea.

The following evening, John, Alexis, and Leo convened at the Lake Worth Drive-In theatre to discuss the heist. It was the only place in Palm Beach County where they could plan and smoke without any interference.

The three accomplices sat inside Leo's new Ford Ranger, smoking blunt after blunt of the finest herb in the county. After hearing their initial talk, Alexis was convinced that John was crazy. But the challenge appealed to him immensely, and he couldn't deny it. Leo was just there to make sure his little brother did not go about things in a stupid fashion. He was also attracted to the entire criminal and financial aspects of the heist.

"Okay, I think the first thing we need to do is inspect the place. We should go there a few times to scope it out," said Alexis, who was sitting in the front passenger seat as the movie played an immense screen in front of the car.

"I was thinking the same thing. I've been there a couple of times when I was a kid. I think the card used to be on the second floor," said John, who was sitting on the cabin's rear foldout seat. He then realized how fogged the car was with weed smoke and said. "Oh shit, do you guys see how fogged it is?"

It was almost pitch-black inside the truck's cabin. Leo turned on the roof lights to confirm the fog's thickness.

"Oh shit, I can barely see you, little dude," giggled Leo to Alexis.

"Yeah, I can't see shit," said John. Alexis became paranoid and opened the window to release some of the smoke. Although there were no police in sight, he was paranoid that the fog would somehow get them in trouble.

"No!" said Leo to Alexis before coughing up a lung. "Close that shit!"

Alexis listened to his big brother and closed the window. Leo then turned off the light, and they continued to discuss the heist.

"Anyways," said Alexis before being distracted by the irony of the film they were watching... "Isn't it funny that we're seeing a movie about a group of guys who are trying to steal from a casino?"

"That is pretty fucking weird," replied a humored John.

"So, what was I saying?" said Alexis as he took a hit from the blunt. "Oh, right... we need to find a way inside. We need to get familiar with that place and find where it's vulnerable."

"We also need to make sure that the card is really there and that it's not some replica. I don't want to go through all this effort for nothing," added Leo.

"Yup," replied Alexis. "And after that, we should check out the surrounding area to plan an escape route."

John was impressed by the Garcia brother's ability to outline an initial plan without much effort. They all grew up in an upper-middle-class lifestyle and attended some of the best catholic schools in South Florida. But that did not mean they weren't thugs, delinquents. For as long as young men like John, Alexis, and Leo could remember, they were always breaking the law in one way or another. Now that they were technically adults, the baseball card heist provided an opportunity to enter a higher level of crime. Whether they had the intellect to do that was yet to be determined.

"The one thing I've been thinking of is... how are we going to get rid of it," said John. It was an imperative point to address, and the Garcia brothers knew it. Alexis was creative, and Leo had his distribution skills. Together, they would need to produce an intelligent escape and sales plan.

"Let's go check the place out, and then we'll see where we go from there," replied Alexis. At that point, the car was so fogged up that neither Leo nor John could see him. They could only hear his voice.

"Little dude! Where are you?" joked Leo.

After returning to the Garcia house, John drove himself out of the neighborhood and onto Boynton Beach Boulevard. As he arrived at the traffic light on Hagen Ranch road, his phone rang. It was an unusual call from his mother, who never called so late. He answered the phone and heard her voice in distress.

"Oh my God! He's dying! He's dying! Johnny! He's dying!"

"What the fuck!? What!?" replied a worried John. "Mom! Slow down. What are you saying? Who's dying?"

"Oh no, Johnny! He's going to die...," replied his mother, who was hysterical and crying.

"Who, Mom!?" asked John.

"Onni! He overdosed on something and is passed out on the floor. He's not breathing."

"Did you call the ambulance?" replied John.

"Yes, yes..."

"Okay, I'm right around the corner. I'll be right there, Mom," assured John.

John arrived at the neighborhood within a few minutes and sped into a parking space, almost hitting another car in the process.

He got out, ran to the door, and opened it. There, on the living room floor, he saw his mother's Finnish husband in a pale blue color.

John's mother was sitting over him, unable to contain her sadness. As John thought of something to do, the ambulance arrived and proceeded to perform treatment on Onni. They attempted to revive him but had little luck.

"Miss, do you know what he took?" asked one of the paramedics.

She handed him a bottle of Xanax and said, "This was almost full last night. I think he drank down the pills with a bottle of Jack Daniels."

Onni was taken to the emergency room at JFK hospital in an ambulance. As soon as it arrived, the doctors and staff strolled away his near-lifeless body on a stretcher.

John and Betsy arrived a few minutes later. They entered the ER waiting room and took a seat. Betsy could barely contain her anxiety. John did his best to console her.

"He's going to be alright, Mom... Onni's gonna pull through, Mom," he would say.

Meanwhile, John was trying to contact his brother, but Vincent could not be reached. It was always impossible to get a hold of him. That made John resent his younger brother and hold him accountable for being a distant member of the family. After trying multiple times, he almost smashed his phone on the ground.

After almost two hours of waiting, the doctor finally arrived to address John's mom. She was a young doctor, attractive, of Hindi descent with a calm demeanor.

"Hi, Mrs. Thibault. I am Doctor Cardoso. I've been working on your husband's case. The good news is that he is alive and breathing through a respirator. But his body underwent a lot of stress, and we need to see how he recovers. So, he will need some time until we know the extent of the damage. The next twenty-four hours are critical."

"Is he going to die?" asked Betsy.

"It's hard to say right now," replied the doctor. "But he is stable."

"What kind of a fucking response is that?" replied Betsy, who was confused and agitated.

"I'm sorry. Right now, we just have to sit and wait. We will do everything we can to help see him through this. Excuse me," said Doctor Torres before walking away.

"Hey, don't walk away from me! Tell me what's wrong with my husband! Who the fuck do you think you are!?" yelled Betsy in a blind rage. "Fucking spic doctor! You're nothing! You're nothing!"

John was smart enough to know the doctor wasn't Hispanic. But then he looked at the people in the waiting room and noticed that many of them were. He was embarrassed by his mother's actions and knew he needed to take her out of there immediately.

"Mom, I think we need to let them monitor Onni. They know what they're doing," said John as he calmly tried to direct his mother towards the exit.

That was when Betsy decided to pull away from her son. She was adamant about getting more information from the medical staff.

"Let me go! Let me go!" she yelled.

Betsy then noticed all the people in the waiting room with concerned looks on their faces. Her own embarrassment led to a prideful rant, first in her mind, then towards the people.

"I'm not crazy. They're crazy. Why were they looking at me with their weird faces? Stupid minorities," she thought.

She pointed at a mother with two little girls, one who looked weak and frail, and said, "Why are all of you looking at me? Huh!?" John froze from the shame. None of the people in the waiting room said anything to trigger his mother. Their humility and silence only enraged her even more.

"Don't look at me like that, you fucking spics! Go back to your country and quit taking our jobs!" she ranted. That was the point when a security guard arrived.

"Miss, I'm going to have to ask you to leave," said the mighty-looking Haitian man.

"I'm sorry, sir. We were just leaving," said John as he put both hands on his delirious mother and escorted her out the door.

When John went to work the next morning, he didn't know if Onni was alive. Just as he was leaving his neighborhood, Vincent arrived home. John slowed down his car and waved at his brother to stop. Vincent stopped and rolled down his window. John noticed that his brother was still wired from a long night of partying.

"Hey," said Vincent.

"Where the fuck have you been? Onni OD'd on Mom's pills

last night. He might fucking die," said John.

"Oh fuck, I was at the Seminole Casino all night, down in Miami. A few of us went after work," replied Vincent. "Don't you have school today?" replied John.

"Yeah, but I was planning on not going in today," replied the high-school senior.

After giving Vincent a few seconds to process his thoughts, John said, "Aren't you even going to ask about Mom?"

"Yeah, I'm going inside to see her," said absent-minded Vincent.

John rolled his eyes and continued driving to work. When he got there, he saw the new hire, Shannon, standing at the doorway with a lost look on her face. He parked his car and sprayed body deodorizer all over his clothes. He took off his faded, disgusting hat and looked in the mirror. He got out of the car, wearing his shades, and retrieved his backpack from the rear seat.

Shannon noticed him from the moment he stepped out of the car and watched as he crossed the road. She had anticipated seeing him since the last time they spoke.

"Hey, I got this," said John as he took out the store keys from his bag.

"Thanks," she uttered out of nervousness.

"How long have you been here?" asked John as he opened the door for her.

"Like, ten minutes. I figured someone would come eventually," she said with a delightful smile.

"Oh, thank you," she said before walking inside the building. There was a second set of doors to pass, and Shannon held one open for John. "After you."

"Thanks," said John as he entered the bookstore and turned on the lights. He appreciated the charm of those first seconds of the day, when the store was silent and empty, and the smell of fresh books coursed through the air.

"So, where will you be working?" he asked.

"I'm in the management training program. So, I'll be involved in a little bit of everything. You work in the music section, right?" replied Shannon.

"Yeah, it's nice and quiet back there most of the time," was all John could say about that place.

"So, how are you liking Florida?" he asked.

"It's really nice. I'm going to FAU to finish my degree in sociology, and it's nice not to have to worry about the cold or snow," replied Shannon with light humor. "And you said that you've been here all of your life?"

"That's right. I went to school here. My whole family lives here. My friends are here. Now, I'm just working, figuring out the next step."

There was a short pause after John spoke. Both were caught in the spell of allurement. John knew it was a moment not to waste. He found it ironic that they were there together, alone, after the horrible night he had. Their morning encounter dulled the sadness he was feeling.

"If you want, I can show you around town sometime," he

offered.

Shannon was flattered and intrigued, but she could not reply the way that John had hoped.

"I'm sorry. I have a boyfriend. We live together in Lake Worth... but thank you." It was not as easy as she thought it would be to say that. She could not deny that the interest was mutual.

John felt rejected and somewhat stupid. But it was not the first time he hit on a girl, and it would not be the last. He also knew he was not finished with Shannon. His faith led him to believe that she could be part of a divine plan. It was simply the way he felt. No matter how dark his world was, the light of God was always present, and his faith was never broken. That was John Thibault in a nutshell.

Chapter Seven

The three bandidos arrived at the Delray Sports Museum the following day to do surveillance. They stepped out of Alexis' Pontiac in a typical cloud of smoke and observed the building's windowpane esthetics.

They all wore shades and reeked of ganja. While walking casually into the building, Alexis immediately noticed an admission fee sign hanging above the register. Behind the register was a young man, a light-skinned African American, waiting for their payment.

John worked, but his pay was miserable, so he was broke. Alexis had no job and lived off his parents. That meant Leo had to pay with his drug-dealing money.

"Aww, you broke-asses are going to make me pay. Aren't you?" said a disappointed Leo.

"I'll get you back," said John with audacity. But Leo knew better. He knew he would never see that money from him.

"Man, shut the fuck up," replied upset Leo. He searched his pockets for his wallet while muttering quietly, "This is fucking bullshit... can't believe I gotta pay for you assholes."

"I told you, I'll pay you back, fat boy," insisted John.

"Shut up!" snapped Leo. "You're not gonna pay me shit," he grumbled while counting his folded-up cash with his thumb, the way only drug dealers count cash.

The museum was three floors of sports greatness, a sports fan's paradise. The inconceivable variety of memorabilia touched each visitor in a special way. Leo walked directly to the football items for gridiron glory. Alexis preferred the boxing collectibles of the great champions of the past. John could only focus on the hockey section.

Alexis could not close his mouth as he stared at the Evander Holyfield memorabilia. It was his favorite fighter of all time, and the museum had signed items from all his big fights. There were also signed shorts, gloves, fight programs, and framed pictures from all the eras of the past.

John paid close attention to the hockey sticks that were signed by legends such as Gretzky, Orr, and Howe. He wanted to add to his collection, which included a signed jersey from the entire 1996 Florida Panthers team. It was the only time they ever got to the finals, and John always carried the memory in his heart.

After the allurement wore off, Alexis and Leo looked for cameras and sensors. They checked every corner of the building, within the frames on the wall, behind some of the racks, on the ceiling, everywhere.

Certain cameras, like the ones at the entrance and on the ceiling, were obvious. But Leo was sure there were others hidden within the glamour. So, he paid attention to odd spots to see if anything unusual caught his attention.

To their advantage, almost everything was displayed in the open. The only concrete walls were on the east side of the building, where each floor had a special viewing area. Also, there was no security guard on site. Everyone could hear a man talking business from a first-floor office. But other than a couple of workers, there was nobody else there.

The boys strolled up the open staircase to the second floor. That was where the sports art was kept. There were hundreds of sports-themed oil paintings on display, including a giant painting of Muhammad Ali shadowboxing underwater. There was also a signed painting of Cal Ripken's iron man moment and a signed painting of the 1927 Yankees team picture.

"Yo, I don't see this card," said pessimistic Leo. "Where the fuck is it?"

"It was on the second floor, but I think they moved it to the third floor," said John.

"Are you sure it's even here?" asked a frustrated Leo. He did not like surprises.

"Calm down, just follow me," said a confident John.

They took the staircase to the third floor, which was mostly dedicated to baseball memorabilia. Once there, Alexis felt like he was in baseball heaven. They were surrounded by the greatest collection of paintings, pictures, and other precious items from every era of baseball history.

The museum's layout guided them directly to their target. John could see the Honus Wagner display on the other side of the third floor. So, he took the lead and casually made his way toward it. They took position around the display case and were awed at the card's simplicity.

"It's so fucking small," said Alexis at first glance. "But it looks exactly like the copies I had as a kid."

"That shit's worth how much?" asked Leo.

"Two-mil," said John.

"You think that's the real card?" asked Alexis.

"Yeah, I think so," replied John. "It's the same case I saw the other day at the Swap Shop. We just have to find out if the old man stores it somewhere at night," said John.

"Yeah, we don't want a switch-a-roo. We need to find out for sure," said Alexis.

They continued to survey the area while pretending to be casual customers. Alexis had the idea of looking for alternative entrances and exits. He eventually spotted a hatch door situated on the roof and could not take his eye off it.

"That's it. That's how we're getting in here," he said to himself.

They walked down the stairs to the first floor, where Mr. Herb Bowman was having a conversation with the front door attendee. He looked up and eyeballed the boys as they walked down the stairs. Normally, Hispanics would lure his attention the most. But this time, he could not take his eyes off the white boy.

"Excuse me," said Herb to grab John's attention.

The boys turned around, giving Herb a chance to clearly look at their faces. Then he said to John, "Hey, Swap Shop, right?"

"Um, yeah, that's right," said a terrified John.

"I never forget a face," he said with skepticism. "Did you guys like what you saw?"

"Yeah, nice collection," said Alexis.

"Pretty cool," said Leo.

"I suddenly have an interest in this stuff again. It's a really impressive collection," said John.

"Yeah, well, this stuff is all mine, and it's all for sale. So, only come back if you have money to spend, okay?" said Herb. It was a less-subtle way of telling them never to return. Herb may have been a nerdy collector, but he was from the South Side of Chicago and knew when three little shits with too much time on their hands were scoping out his business.

Instead of letting his emotions take control, Leo decided not to reply to the old man. On any other occasion, he would have sent the man to hell or threatened violence. But for the sake of the heist, he decided to get out of there as quickly as possible.

"That was not fucking cool," said Leo after they exited the museum.

"Yeah, that guy knows who we are now," said Alexis before noticing the Intracoastal neighborhood behind the museum.

"It's fine, fuck him," replied John.

Alexis put the key in the keyhole of his car. But he did not open the door without making something clear.

"There's three of us. We did what we needed to do. And now we gotta plant some cameras in that fucking place. After all this, we're not stopping, and he's not stopping us."

"I'm going to fucking choke you. Get in the car and get me outta here," was all Leo said before he sat into the car.

On the ride home, the boys were all reflecting on the heist in their own unique way. The challenge was grand, and they all had ideas to make it a successful attempt. Alexis kept focusing on the neighborhoods that ran along the east side of Federal Highway. He realized that those homes sat along the Intracoastal Waterway, which made him think of an escape plan.

"Hey, I'm turning around," said Alexis as they got to Linton Boulevard.

"What do you mean? Why?" asked John.

"I want to check out the neighborhood behind the museum," said Alexis.

"For what?" said John.

"I'll tell you when we get there so that it makes sense," replied Alexis.

He drove back towards the museum. But instead of turning into the parking lot, he drove down a street next to the museum that led to one of the Intracoastal neighborhoods.

"Let's stop right here," said Alexis before stepping out of the car. John and Leo had no idea what he was thinking.

"Where the fuck is he going?" asked Leo.

Alexis walked to a large hedge, observed its location, and returned to the car. He approached Leo's passenger-side window to explain his reasoning.

"Those hedges are the only thing that separates the museum from this neighborhood. And about a quarter mile down that street is the Intracoastal," said Alexis while pointing east.

"So, what's your point?" asked John.

"That's how we're escaping. We'll set up a few bikes along

this bush the night of the robbery. Once we grab this thing, we get the fuck out, cross the bushes, grab the bikes, and ride to the water. Once we're there, we dump the bikes and take a boat to a safe spot," said Alexis.

"Where are we going to get a boat from?" asked Leo, who thought the plan sounded somewhat legitimate.

"There's only one person I know with a boat," said Alexis.

"Who?" asked John.

"Brian," said Alexis.

"And then what?" asked Leo.

"Well, if Brian lets us use his boat for a cut, we can head out to a remote location to meet a buyer before the morning news announces the robbery. But that's one thing we have to do, find a buyer who will pay for this shit. If we reduce our margin significantly, we can flip it quickly and walk away with a lot of money," explained Alexis.

"That's actually not a bad idea. The cops will be busy locking down streets instead of looking on the water," said John. "So, where do we go from here, Guapos?"

"We need to plant some micro cameras in that place. There's this spy shop in Miami that sells a bunch of shit like that. Once we get all the equipment we need, we'll find out where the fuck this old guy stores the card and create a plan of attack. Then we need to set off the alarm. We gotta test it and find out how long it takes the cops to get here."

"And, when the fuck do you plan on actually breaking into the place?" said Leo.

"New Year's... considering everything that happened recently in New York, I have a feeling that cops will be on high alert at places where people gather, like downtown. But even then, when the ball drops, there's a window when nearly everyone gets distracted. So, I think we should do it at midnight. At the same time, we can have an alibi."

"You guys are fucking crazy," said Leo. "You're going to get caught. It's a stupid idea, and I don't think it's worth the risk."

"If one-point-five million isn't worth the risk, then I don't know what is," said Alexis. He knew that he had his brother's attention after saying that.

"When was the last time you spoke to Brian?" asked John.

"Since he left for UNF. But that motherfucker kind of owes me. So, I don't see why he can't do this. I mean, as long as he's not on house arrest or anything," said Alexis.

They made plans to meet the following evening to test the alarm system. The Garcia brothers dropped off John at his apartment and went home. When John walked inside, he saw Onni lying on the couch, pretending like he was sleeping. His mother walked out of the bedroom with a basket of linens that needed to be washed.

Although there was awkwardness in the ambiance, John was glad to see her being productive.

"How's Onni?" he asked.

"Still out of it, but the doctor says he should recover like normal in a week or two," replied Betsy.

"Are you feeling better?" he asked while still standing at the doorway.

"Yeah, thanks. I called work and told them I'd be in tomorrow," said Betsy before returning to her room to grab the rest of the laundry.

John looked at Onni and felt a notch of disgust in his gut. He detested the sight of a jobless immigrant sprawled on his couch. After seven years since Onni entered their lives, John thought he was a pathetic man unworthy of his mother.

"So, is Onni still going to look for work?" John asked Betsy. She hated every time John asked that.

"When are you going to give him a break? He's been through enough," replied Betsy.

"When he stops all this bullshit and gets a fucking job," said John before walking to his room. He changed his shirt and grabbed his bookbag before leaving the apartment for another shift at the bookstore.

Chapter Eight

John stepped into the bookstore and walked quickly to the back, hoping to avoid any sort of human engagement with customers or co-workers. The heist was weighing heavily on his mind, and he wanted the day to pass as quickly as possible. But to his surprise, he arrived at the music section and saw Shannon attending to a customer. Seeing that quickly changed his mind about human interaction for the day.

At first, John took time to observe her from the counter. Her milky skin and gentle eyes formed a classic look that he found irresistible. When she was finished with the customer, Shannon walked to the counter to greet John.

"Hi, John!" she said.

"Hey, Shannon! What brings you to this side?" he asked.

"Tanisha asked me to shadow you today. I think she wants me to see how the section operates," replied Shannon. "Are you okay with that?"

"Me? Sure, that's not a problem," he replied. "Do you want to help me stack these new DVDs?"

"Sure, let's do it," she replied pleasantly.

John carried a box of DVDs to the film section while Shannon calmly followed him. He was nervous about exposing his chaotic life to her. But he was interested enough to start a productive conversation.

"I'll put away these, and you put away the rest;' said John as he took three large stacks out of the box. "Just find the genre and go by alphabetical order."

They were a productive tandem from the start. Working diligently while carrying on a pleasant conversation. John decided to use the opportunity to find out more about her. Shannon replied as best as she could, trying not to kill the mood by talking about her boring life back in New Jersey. But she appreciated the platonic encounter. It allowed her to think about something other than her personal problems.

After stacking the DVDs, John and Shannon attended to customers at the register. The third customer, a snowbird in her seventies who looked like she had just arrived from the beach, shared an honest observation.

"I've been watching you two from the back of the line. Are you dating?" she asked, all fresh.

John and Shannon both became flushed with embarrassment. Neither could immediately conjure a response.

"Well, I know good chemistry when I see it. My husband and I have been married for fifty years because we get along just the same way," said the kind-hearted woman.

The old woman left, and the co-workers found themselves alone in the music section. The attraction was growing by the second, and there were still four hours left in the shift. John continued to watch his words, putting more effort as a listener than a talker. Shannon appreciated that.

"So, John, do you really not have a girlfriend?" asked Shannon. She thought he was too nice to be single. "Why do you say that?" replied John.

"Because you asked me out, leading me to assume that you're not with anybody," replied Shannon.

"No, I'm not seeing anyone. Right now, I'm just trying to work as much as I can and save as much money as possible," replied John.

"Saving up for anything particular?" asked Shannon.

"Not really, but I am trying to move out on my own. I still live with my mom. But that's getting old because her husband lives there too."

"You mean your stepdad?" she replied.

"No, he isn't anything to me," replied John, who quickly wanted to change the subject. "So, where do you and your boyfriend live?"

"We're renting an efficiency in Greenacres. The place is kind of a dump and dangerous. So, I'm hoping to leave as soon as possible," she said openly. The comment made John wonder if she was sending him a hidden message, like she was not happy with her relationship.

"That's a tough part of town. There're some safe and cheap apartments here in Boynton. I can show you around if you'd like," said John. It became apparent to Shannon that he was a persistent person.

"Um, I don't think he'd like that," she replied with a charmed smile.

She expected John to give a disappointed reaction, but there was none. He only turned his head and continued to document the inventory. Shannon had no intentions of losing his interest and redirected the conversation to find out more about him.

"Do you like working here?" she asked.

"It's just a job. Most of the time, I'm here by myself. Sometimes I hang out with the café people. They're pretty cool. But I'm not the biggest fan of retail, especially during the season. There's a lot of miserable people who come into the store just to make trouble," he replied.

"Yeah, I see how that can be a problem. I'm not one for interactions. I try to stay away from socializing as much as possible," said Shannon.

Their personalities gravitated closer and closer throughout the day. In an instant, John felt as though he had met the woman of his life. Despite her being in a relationship, he knew they were meant for each other. Coincidentally, Shannon felt the same.

Over at the cafeteria, Angelica wondered why John hadn't arrived. She worked through an entire shift without taking a break, just to be free when John took his break. But he never appeared. She felt in her gut that it had something to do with the new girl.

The wait eventually became unbearable withstand. After finishing the evening rush, she left the café in search of John. While walking through the book sections, she considered the disappointment of seeing John and Shannon happily together. The idea caused a disturbing feeling in her gut. And as she turned out of the book aisle, her worst fears were confirmed. Angelica saw John and Shannon standing close together, having what she thought to be an unprofessional interaction.

She watched in secret and noticed John's expression when he talked to Shannon. She had never seen such an innocent smile from him. Around her, he always held the same depressed look on his face. And then Shannon looked up and noticed Angelica watching them.

"Hey, mister, where have you been all night? I thought we were taking a break together?" she said in her cutest tone to confront the awkwardness of getting caught. John immediately found her presence to be a nuisance.

"I didn't know we were taking a break together," he said. She replied by just gasping in playful disbelief.

"Have you met Shannon?" John asked Angelica.

"Don't change the subject. You have some explaining to do, mister," she said without acknowledging Shannon. That was when John became overly annoyed by her immaturity.

"I don't owe you anything. Shannon, this is Angelica. She works in the café," said John.

Shannon extended her hand, but Angelica refused to focus on anything other than John. She just kept staring at him all wide-eyed.

"Well? I'm not letting you off the hook," she said. "Sorry, Angelica, we don't have time for this. I'm training Shannon. I'll call you later," said John.

"Fine! I forgive you, but you still owe me," she replied before walking away and never shaking Shannon's hand.

"Owe you?" said John as she left the music section.

Angelica had officially made the situation awkward for John and Shannon. But they soon returned to their chat and became lost in time. Both were in disbelief when they realized that closing time was approaching, and neither wanted the shift to end. John could not remember the last time he felt so at peace. Shannon had ignited a lost sense of hope in his life, something he was desperately looking for.

Chapter Nine

While John was enthralled in his love interests at the bookstore, Alexis was working on securing a boat. He arrived at Three-Sandy's restaurant on the Intracoastal and walked to the bar for a meeting. Three-Sandy's was located across from The Yellow Tail restaurant in the Boynton Marina. It was considered by many as the more fun version of the Thibault family restaurant.

Alexis walked through the crowd, looking for a familiar face. But it was hard to make distinctions at that point. The environment was loud and somewhat rowdy. He arrived at the middle of the bar, where a bald character was surrounded by a group of drunk women on the prowl. It was obvious to Alexis that those women sought the skinhead's attention, but he wasn't giving it to anyone. He was just drinking his beer in solace.

Alexis tapped the bald guy on the shoulder and said, "Hey, man. Don't you notice all these women around you?"

"Na, them bitches are too old," said Brian Saunders with a smile. He was Alexis's longest-known yet estranged friend. "Sit down, dude? Where the fuck have you been?" he added.

Alexis pulled out his fake I.D. and waived down the bartender. The gorgeous blonde walked his way and said, "What can I get you, babe?"

"Let me have a Brew House," he replied. Meanwhile, Brian was still waiting for a reply.

"One Brew House, you got it," she replied with a wink and a smile.

"So, what's up? I've been around here, going to school. How's UNF?" replied Alexis loudly to talk over the crowd.

Brian took a fast chug of his beer to show what he had learned at college. He slammed the glass and burped vigorously.

"Jacksonville is the shit. But it's nice to be back here for the holidays. How come you haven't come up?" asked Brian.

"Been busy here with school and some other shit. You still kicking?" bluntly asked Alexis regarding Brian's drug dealings.

"Yep, there's a lot of business up there. Making about ten G's a month right now. I sell to all those students, in the dorms, off campus, and even to teachers," replied boastful Brian.

The bartender brought Alexis his beer, and the two old friends touched glasses.

"Cheers to good times," said Alexis.

"Cheers, bro," said Brian. "You still talk to John?"

"Yeah... that dude's funny. Still drinking like a fish and smoking a box of cigarettes a day. We've actually been working on a little project lately."

"What kind of project?" said Brian with a sarcastic grin on his face.

"I'll tell you about it later. Let's get drunk first," replied Alexis.

They had a profound history as friends. Alexis and Brian were partners in crime during middle school. Out of boredom, they would break into houses and steal bicycles. They shared similar, hardcore interests, and both lost their virginities on the same night at the same party. From the age of nine to the age of sixteen, Alexis and Brian were always up to no good. Therefore, they spent a good portion of that evening reminiscing about old debaucheries, laughing hysterically at all the stupidities they did. Beer after beer, the laughter got louder until they both had beat-red faces.

"Oh, shit! I can't believe you remember that. Bro, you were so fucked up. We couldn't wake you up. Nobody knows what happened after we threw you into the bathroom with the hooker. We just heard a bunch of moaning and talking," said Alexis.

"That girl was kind of nasty. Remember, she had that bandage hanging from her back. She could've had AIDS," said Brian in deep thought. "She tried sucking me off, but I just passed out. When I woke up, she was getting dressed and leaving."

"Is that why you chased her out the door?" asked Alexis.

"Yeah, she still had all our money. I wanted her to finish," said Brian.

"It was hilarious. She threatened to take out her knife when you asked for the money. I thought you were gonna do something stupid," said Alexis.

"I wanted to. Then you started preaching bible verses to her. You were like trying to save her after she made you bust a nut," recollected Brian.

"Oh yeah, that's right. Then that fucking pimp came and showed us his gun. We're lucky he didn't rob us. He was actually pretty cool by giving us some of our money back," said Alexis before drinking more of his beer. "I think he just wanted to get out of there," he slurred.

The evening continued in drunkard conversation. They may

have only been nineteen, but both had enough life-experience to merit a seat at any bar. They spoke of the old gang, the ones whose lives spiraled out of control and the ones who were no longer alive. Some died of drug overdoses; others died of suicide. Some were in jail, while others joined the military or became parents. The endless directions of life staked a claim to each young soul from their past.

They were all Catholic school kids from the diocese of Palm Beach County. John, Alexis, and Brian all attended the same high school and remained close friends until Alexis was expelled Junior year. After that, Alexis and John remained friends, and Brian became a fast-paced drug dealer.

After four pitchers of beer, Alexis and Brian left the bar to smoke a cigarette. They stood dockside along the Intracoastal, watching two boats go under the Ocean Avenue Bridge. The moonlight shimmered over the water ripples they left behind.

"Remember when we used to take acid and jump off that shit? John's grandpa would get so pissed," said Alexis.

"We were fucking... scaring away the customers," said Brian as he took a drag.

"Yo, man," we gotta talk about some shit... John and I are pulling a two-million-dollar heist. Our escape plan requires a boat. You're the only guy I know who could help us," said Alexis in a direct manner.

"What the fuck? What do you mean? Explain this heist to me," said the drunk and cynical drug dealer.

"So, John, Leo, and I are going after a two-million-dollar baseball card. We're breaking into the sports museum in Delray.

It's right on Federal Highway. There's a street behind it that leads to the water. I need you to pick us up at that spot after we've taken the card," said Alexis.

Brian took a deep breath to absorb what he was hearing.

"And where would I be taking you?" he asked.

"Either to a drop-off point down the way or to the buyer. I'm still working on that pare replied Alexis. "This is insane. How the hell do you plan on stealing that card? You said it's in a museum?"

"Yeah, the sports museum in Delray. But don't worry about that. All I need from you is a boat ride. If you can do that, we'll cut you in for ten thousand," said Alexis. "What do you think?"

Brian was at a loss for words. The idea sounded nice. But he couldn't rationalize it. "Alexis... I gotta go home and think about this. It sounds impossible. When do you plan on doing this?"

"New year's, midnight," affirmed Alexis.

"There's definitely going to be patrol out on the water at that time. It sounds too risky," said Brian.

"Look, just think about it and let me know. Otherwise, I gotta come up with another plan," said Alexis.

Brian was humored by the entire evening. He was happy to share a beer with his old friend Alexis. He was grateful for the opportunity.

"It's good to see you, bro. All things aside, I've been wanting to talk to you for a long time about what happened before I left," said Brian.

"You know what, man? Let's just forget about it. But if you

want to make things up to me, do us this favor," replied Alexis. He paused for a second before continuing. "For what it's worth, you still have a friend in me. I know a bunch of shit happened, but I'm glad to see you too."

Chapter Ten

With little time to waste, Leo drove John and Alexis to a spy shop on Miami Beach. John wasn't familiar with Miami-Dade County. Most residents of Palm Beach County weren't. After passing Oakland Park, lifelong Palm Beachers like John felt out of the protection of suburbia.

The Garcia brothers lived in Miami for three years before moving to Palm Beach County. They were familiar with the tri-county area. Therefore, John took a backseat, literally and figuratively, as the Garcia brothers navigated the journey south to get supplies. After passing Star Island on the left, they continued east towards Washington Avenue, where the shop was located.

"Hey, how much money did you bring?" Alexis asked Leo while walking to the shop.

"Man, don't worry about it. I'm good," replied Leo. "You two broke asses better pay me back for this shit. I work hard for my money."

"By what? Selling weed?" sarcastically asked John, who was smoking a cigarette.

"Exactly, the same weed that got you high on the way here and will get you high on the way back," said Leo as they arrived at the shop.

"Here it is," said Alexis before opening the door.

They were out of their element. None of them were tech-geeks or knew anything about surveillance. The entire operation was based on what they had seen on television, usually in action movies. Everything in that store looked ridiculously expensive, and it was not guaranteed they would find the cameras they needed.

The store owner, a massive Ukrainian immigrant, noticed the boys from the moment they arrived. He thought they looked lost and out of place. As Alexis and John were looking at larger security cameras on the display rack, he approached them to assist.

"Gentleman, can I help you with something?" he said with a thick Ukrainian accent.

"Hi, yeah, we're looking for mini cameras. Something that can be hidden," said Alexis, who was still wearing his shades.

"These aren't what you need. Follow me," said the Ukrainian.

John, Alexis, and Leo walked to a display rack on the other side of the store and were presented with a full collection of mini cameras. Alexis could not believe they had exactly what he was looking for. He gazed at the options that were available, hoping they were within his budget.

"I think you would be more interested in these. They run on lithium batteries and everything records on the SD card. You can set it to record video or take pictures," said the informative owner.

"So, how are these priced?" asked Leo.

"The cheapest ones are here to the left. The more expensive ones are here to the right," said the owner. "This one here is the cheapest at fifty dollars."

Alexis looked at Leo to see his reaction. He didn't seem to mind the price. The cameras were far less expensive than he anticipated. But Leo thought they were only looking for two or three cameras.

"How many do you need?" asked the owner as he leaned against the glass counter.

"I think we'll need five," replied Alexis.

"Aww, fuck," expressed Leo with aggressive intolerance. "That's going to be almost three hundred dollars."

"Hey! I told you, we'll pay you back," said John in a stern tone.

"Man....," Leo could hardly express his next sentence out of frustration. He had to hold back from punching John. "Just shut the fuck up... you're not going to pay me shit... fucking white devil."

Leo took out his wallet and paid for the five cameras in cash. The Ukrainian kindly bagged their items, and the boys left the shop. The next stop was a sporting goods store in Doral. Leo drove across the 836 highway to west Dade as John smoked cigarettes and Alexis read the camera's instruction manual.

The store was located in the Dolphin Mall. John and Leo followed Alexis inside the store and towards the outdoors section. There, Alexis quickly located the steel grappling hooks, climbing rope, and harnesses.

"I think we're going to have to get in through the roof. I figured we could use these to get up there," explained Alexis.

"This is getting ridiculous. Who the fuck's going to climb up there?" asked Leo.

"No, no, this is a great idea. If we get in through the roof, maybe we can bypass the alarms and sensors," said John.

"I guess John and I will," said Alexis to his brother. "Your fat ass is going to have to drop us off with the bikes and then leave the car at the Publix. Then you'll have to walk back to the bikes. By that time, we'll already be on the roof. At midnight, we'll pop the hatch, get in, and get out."

"Alright, just *get* what you need and make sure to save the receipts. I got a feeling this is all going to fizzle out, and I want to get my money back when it does," said pessimistic Leo.

"Again, with the money; that's all you care about, money, money, money, money," complained John to purposely test Leo's patience.

"Shut...the fuck...up!" growled Leo to John. Nothing pleased John more than getting a reaction from short-tempered Leo.

They put the items in a shopping cart and proceeded to the checkout line. The cashier at the register had an awkwardly cheerful expression on his face.

"You guys going rock climbing?" said the pimple-faced teen.

"Something like that," replied stoned Alexis, who was not in the mood for conversation.

"Well, what else could it be? I mean, who are you? Mission impossible?" he replied with a smart mouth.

"Dude, it's none of your fucking business. Can you just give me the receipt?" replied Alexis. The cashier noted Alexis's tone and quickly ended the transaction.

They returned to Leo's truck and headed north on the Turnpike to Palm Beach County. One hour later, they pulled into a gas station that was down the street from the sports museum. Leo parked the truck, and Alexis stepped outside with a screwdriver in hand. He quickly removed the truck's license plate to hide its identity.

"So, what exactly are we going to do?" asked Leo.

"Well, I'm going to throw this big rock that I have through one of the store's windows. It should set off the alarm. Then we're going to chill across the street and time how long it takes the cops to show up," said Alexis.

"You're really going to break the fucking window?" asked John from the back seat.

"Yep, really quick. It's important we do this," said Alexis.

Leo left the gas station and drove to the sports museum. It was closed for the evening, so there was nobody in the parking lot. Alexis directed Leo to drive to the hedges in the back of the lot to indicate the escape route.

"There it is. Look how quickly we can hide ourselves as soon as we go through the hedges," said Alexis.

"You got a point, Guapos," said John.

"But first, let's see how much time we'll have," continued Alexis before wrapping a shirt around his face.

Under the dark of night, Leo pulled in front of the museum's entrance door. Alexis picked up the cinderblock, stepped out of the truck, and walked up to the glass building. He could see inside and noticed the Honus Wagner display on the third floor. As far as he could tell, none of the display items had been put away.

Without further hesitation, Alexis lunged at the cinderblock with all his strength at the glass wall. To his surprise, the cinderblock bounced off the hurricane-proof glass and almost knocked his head off. As the deafening alarm sounded, he noticed that the rock hardly made a scratch on the glass.

"Go into that parking lot across the street and park behind those bushes," said Alexis after getting inside the truck.

"You threw that shit with all your strength, and nothing happened. Those are some powerful windows," said Leo.

He parked the car across the Federal Highway and turned off the lights. Their location provided protection behind Ficus trees but with a clear view of the museum. They sat in the dark while the alarm blasted into the night sky and waited for the police to arrive.

"This is crazy. I can't believe we're doing this," said John.

"I know, but it's worth the try. As-long-as we know where the card is, we have a real shot at getting this done," said Alexis.

"That rock didn't even make a dent. I wasn't expecting that," said John in a low tone, although there was no reason to be quiet.

"You know what that means?" replied Alexis while looking up and down the Federal Highway for the police. "What?" replied John.

"The roof is the only way in and out. Like that kid said, this is going to be some real Mission Impossible shit. But, fuck it... it's kind of a rush," said Alexis.

"Do you guys hear any police sirens?" asked Leo. "I don't hear shit," said John.

"Me neither," said Alexis.

"How long has it been?" asked John.

"Two and a half minutes," said Alexis.

John used the idle time to reveal a minor change in the plans. There was something he'd wanted to reveal to Alexis all day.

"Hey, uh, I forgot to tell you. I can't plant the cameras tomorrow. I got a date," said John.

"With Angelica?" asked Alexis.

"No, with some new girl from work. I think I'm in love, bro," said John.

"Damn, I don't think I've ever heard you say that, not with Cassie, not even with Jenn," replied Alexis.

"Yeah, well, she's also got a friend visiting from Canada. So, you want to hang out with us? Maybe go bowling or something?" said John.

"Mmmmm....," muttered Alexis while staring at the museum. "Canadian puntang? I'm in. But what about Angelica? You done with her?"

"I've been trying to avoid her. She's been calling me all day, but I think it's over. I mean, we were never really together. It was just sex. I didn't want her to fall in love with me, but I think it's too late," said John.

After five minutes of waiting, Leo became impatient. He lit a blunt and took five large hits to get it burning. At the same time, he observed the cars that drove north and south along Federal Highway. But nobody paid attention to the alarm.

"Should we get the fuck out of here?" he asked before passing the blunt.

"Let's see if we can push it to six minutes. The longer they delay, the more time we know we have," replied Alexis.

When the sixth minute came, Leo turned on the ignition and drove off the parking lot. It had been a long and productive day. After returning to the Garcia house, John and Alexis stayed in the driveway to talk about their pending matters. They stood among the five family cars and conversed while admiring the Christmas lights.

"So, you're coming tomorrow?" asked John while smoking another cigarette.

"Yeah, I said I was. Why are you all nervous about this girl?" asked Alexis.

"I don't know. I feel different about her," he said before pushing another topic to avoid talking about his feelings. "Did you talk to Brian?"

"Yeah, I think he's in. He's still the same, so I don't think he'll turn down the money. He also asked about you," replied Alexis.

"Yeah, well, we got to keep an eye on that guy. I don't trust him anymore, not after all the shit I've heard he's into," admitted John.

"I know, me neither. But we need him if we're going to pull this off," replied Alexis.

They finished smoking, and John went home to rest. He arrived at his apartment complex and saw Angelica sitting on the sidewalk under a streetlight. He noticed that she was crying and in distress. After he stepped out of the car, she rose to her feet.

"What's wrong? Why are you crying?" he asked.

"Because you're not... talking to me... anymore," she mumbled. "Everything was great, and now you're so distant. Did I do something wrong?"

"No, Angelica, I've just been working on a project with Alexis. You shouldn't be acting this way," replied John.

"Of course, I should. I love you, John. I know you don't express yourself much, but I know you love me too," said Angelica as dramatically as she could.

"Whoa, look, I really don't think any of this is healthy right now. We're friends, I care for you, but I can't be more than that," said John.

Angelica struggled to process John's honesty. It made her speechless, barely able to sound the next words.

"I... don't even... know you anymore," she replied.

"Look, I have to go inside. I'm not going to leave you like this. Just come in with me," said John. He carefully put his arm around Angelica, and they walked inside the apartment.

John did not speak much the rest of that evening. He certainly did not want to reveal anything about

Shannon. But Angelica had her suspicions, and it did not take long for her to bring up the issue.

John put on a movie to help ease the tension. It was a parody of calamitous highway police officers. Angelica calmed down and became comfortable in his bed. She eventually snuggled her backside against him to ensure his attention. John knew what she was doing, but he could not back away from her lure.

"Do you like the new girl?" said Angelica without warning while staring at the television.

"Can we just watch the movie?" replied John to avoid the subject.

"It's just that... I see the way you look at her. And it's pretty obvious to me that she likes you."

John knew that he was moments away from having sex. He didn't want to ruin that. So, he carefully articulated his next words.

"Angelica, I'm not with anyone right now but you," he said.

She turned around, looked into his eyes, and they engaged in a passionate kiss and stress-relieving sex. When it was over, John found it hard to fall asleep. He stayed up for hours, regretting the intercourse and thinking of Shannon. He thought deeply about her as Angelica breathed lightly on his arm. Then he thought about his mother, his father, and the heist. His mind was running on overdrive as the anxiety mounted. It was so much that he started feeling his young heart racing.

John moved off the bed and sat on his couch to regain composure. For a brief moment, he thought he was having a panic attack. Wearing only his gold cross and underwear, John sunk his head and took five deep breaths.

Chapter Eleven

It was bowling night. John was candidly nurturing a romance with Shannon. At the same time, Alexis was showing off his bowling skills to Shannon's Canadian friend. Other than being a degenerate college student, he was also an ace at all drinking games. And after a few pitchers, he gave the Canadian plenty to ponder.

"Something's got me on point tonight. I think you're good luck, Tina," said Alexis while walking back to his seat. "Your turn."

"Okay, but I think you're going to need to show me how it's done because I just can't seem to get it right," she replied while seductively picking up her ball.

"No problem," replied Alexis as he approached her to assist.

Meanwhile, John and Shannon sat at a table, fostering a relaxing conversation. There was magic in the ambiance, shrouded by infidelity. Despite the circumstances, everything felt in place when they were together. Neither could deny the sense of peace that occurred when they were together.

"So, how long have you guys been friends?" Shannon asked about Alexis.

"I've known Alexis since we were kids. We used to play baseball together for years. Then we went to the same high school and have hung out since," said John.

"I can tell this isn't your first double date together," suggested Shannon.

"Why do you say that?" asked John.

"Because you're both doing so well tonight," replied Shannon while observing her friend getting dried humped on the bowling lane as Alexis showed proper form.

"Is this what you guys do? Lure innocent girls with cheap beer and bowling?" asked Shannon.

"So, I've lured you?" asked John with a charming smile. Shannon blushed before saying, "You sure as heck did something right to get me here."

John appreciated her charm. After seeing that they were out of beer, he asked her to walk with him to the concession stand. He didn't want to disrupt their conversation.

"Can I please have one more pitcher?" John asked the bar girl.

"One more pitcher, you got it," replied the young, tatted worker.

They sat on bar stools to continue their conversation. The environment presented a lively setting that helped ease any nervousness they were feeling.

"So, where's your family? Are they all in Jersey?" asked John.

"Yeah, but my parents are separated. They're going through a divorce right now. That's kind of the reason I came here. I could have stayed at Rutgers, but I really needed to get away."

"And your boyfriend just followed?" asked John.

"Well, yeah, pretty much. He said he would help financially. But since we got here, he hasn't been able to hold a job. And now we just fight all the time," revealed Shannon.

"About what?" asked John.

"Money, time... he thinks I'm not home enough. But I am either working or at school, so I'm not really sure what to do to make him happy," said Shannon.

"Well, it sounds like you're too busy for all that drama. I mean, you're training to be management and finishing school at the same time. That's hard enough as it is," replied John to passively instigate.

"Yeah, he doesn't care about that. Sometimes I think he doesn't want me to finish school," said Shannon.

"That's ridiculous. I'm sorry if I'm overstepping my boundaries, but it sounds like he's holding you back instead of supporting you," added John.

Shannon was happy to hear positive reinforcement for once. Her situation at home had become toxic, and she was looking for a way out.

"So, what about you?" she asked to revert the spotlight. "What are you doing? What are your plans?"

"What do you mean?" asked John.

"I mean, do you plan on staying at Weiss St Fletcher your whole life?" she asked.

John was not sure how to answer the question. He had not settled on a collegiate path and had no interests to pursue at the time. And he certainly wasn't going to tell her about the two-million dollars heist he was attempting. So, he told her a portion of the truth for her safety and his.

"I really don't know. For now, I'll work. School is too expensive. So, I'm not sure if I can ever afford it. I guess I just have to wait and see said John.

The bartender returned with the beer, and John presented his fake I.D. They returned to the lane, and the girls went to the bathroom. John poured two beers as Alexis approached him with a big smile on his face.

"How's it going with Tina?" asked John.

"She's so fucking hot!" he whispered. "This was a great idea."

"Yeah, she wants to fuck you. That's what Shannon said," replied John.

"Really, she said that?" asked Alexis before chugging his beer.

"Yep, so don't fuck this up," advised John.

"Okay, well, then we need to get the fuck out of here," suggested Alexis.

"Let's go back to your place. You said your parents aren't home, right?" said John.

"Right, they're in Orlando. So, it's just Leo and me right now."

The girls returned from the bathroom, and John told them about going to Alexis's house. The girls were on board with the idea, and they left the bowling alley in separate cars. Shannon followed Alexis's car to his parent's house. John packed a bowl for the ride there to enhance the alcohol's effect. He was feeling good, not dreadful or worried. The streetlights radiated into his eyes on the way home, and the motivating energy of the punk rock music illuminated his soul.

They arrived at the neighborhood's security gate, and the guard let Alexis through. Shannon parked on Alexis's driveway, and both girls stepped out of the car. Tina took a minute to admire the home's size.

"Hey, it's this way," said Alexis to the girls.

He guided them through the lavish garden to the home's front door. He let everyone inside, disabled the alarm, and turned on the lights. Shannon and Tina were immediately impressed by the home's modern elegance.

"You have a really nice house, Alexis," whispered Shannon.

"Yeah, your parents must be rich," added Tina, who came from a humbler background.

Alexis refrained from answering. With sex on his mind, he just walked to his father's bar and took out a bottle of rum. He placed it on the kitchen's marble counter, grabbed three cups from the cabinet, and put ice into each cup.

"Are you girls drinking?" he asked as they entered the family room.

Tina nodded her head 'yes,' and Shannon declined.

Alexis poured rum into the cups and added soda. He handed John and Tina their cups before directing them to the back patio. He kept the lights off to maintain a romantic setting for the girls.

They sat on the large, screened patio with a pool and hot tub. Outside of the screened area was a large backyard. Outside of Garcia's property line was nothing but sugar sand and construction equipment. It was a new development with only a few homes that were built.

Everybody walked to the patio table, where John sat next to Shannon and Alexis sat next to Tina. The sounds of the swimming pool waterfall and the everglades insects provided a soothing ambiance under the stars.

"Why do I hear so many different noises?" asked Tina.

"Because that's the sounds of the swamp, Canada. But don't worry, this screen keeps the bugs away," said Alexis.

"What do your parents do?" asked Tina.

"My dad's a dentist. He's got a few practices," replied Alexis.

"This is the castle. His parents always have fiestas where everybody gets wasted," said John while taking out a joint.

"Do you smoke?" John asked Shannon.

"I've tried it a few times, but normally I don't," she said. "I do," mentioned Tina, which made Alexis happier than he already was.

"But I'll try some of the local stuff," said Shannon after changing her mind.

"Are you sure?" asked John.

"Yeah, I've been really stressed lately, and I think this is what I need," replied Shannon.

The four youths sat at the table, basking in the spirit of the atmosphere. John and Alexis worked in tandem to create an entertaining mood. They talked, they laughed, and they educated each other about Florida, New Jersey, and Canada. All the while, Alexis kept going inside the house to serve everybody drinks. And after a couple of trips, Shannon finally asked for one. Although she nursed the single drink for the rest of the evening, it was enough to lower her stress levels drastically.

"Hey, does that hot tub work?" asked Tina.

"Yeah, I just need to flip the switch. Why? You want to go in?" asked Alexis.

"I mean... it's there, it's December, and it's warm. The Canadian girl in me can't look away," said Tina.

"But we don't have bathing suits," reminded Shannon, knowing that her friend didn't mind skinny dipping.

"Now, you know that doesn't mean anything to me," replied Tina. "So, what do you say?" she asked Alexis.

"Uh, I'll be right back," he said before going to the pump to turn on the hot tub.

When he returned, Tina was standing poolside, dipping her toe in the water to check the temperature.

"It'll take a few minutes to warm up," said Alexis as he returned, smiling from cheek to cheek.

"I don't have to wait that long," replied Tina before she took off her shirt, pulled down her pants, and entered the water feet first in her underwear.

After getting over the amazement, Alexis stripped down to his underwear. He stepped into the hot tub and tried to share her same enthusiasm. But the Floridian felt the water was ridiculously cold. Still, he stood next to Tina and started to lightly touch his body against hers as they got used to the water's temperature.

"Let me help you warm up," he told her.

John and Shannon opted to stay dry and continue their conversation at the table. Just like the night at the store, time flew. The essence of the words that were exchanged that evening made it seem like their problems no longer existed.

"This is probably the nicest house I've seen in Florida since I got here," mentioned Shannon.

"Yeah, Guapos's dad has a bunch of degrees. His parents work hard," replied John.

"And Alexis is in school too, right?" asked Shannon. "Yeah, he started taking classes as soon as high school ended," said John before taking a drag of his cigarette.

Shannon was a grand proponent of upper-level education. She couldn't understand how a young person wouldn't use their time to build a foundation for the next fifty years of life. She didn't want to get into too much detail about future goals with John. She was only interested in knowing if he was a motivated person.

"So, how do you feel about school?" she asked

"It's not for me. It's too expensive, and I don't have the money to think about school. Besides, I need to help out my mom these days. So school isn't even an option," said John.

"Isn't there something that you want out of life?" asked Shannon.

"I want to own land... invest in some real estate one day. It's a safe bet. Everything else is hopeless," said John.

Shannon considered emotional intelligence and educational intelligence of equal value. She thought that John's emotional intelligence was extremely high. She admired the way that he always maintained a calm demeanor. So, it was hard for her to accept that someone like him saw education as a hopeless effort.

"You're not really giving yourself much of a chance, Mr. Thibault. I'm not saying that school is for everyone, but it's certainly not a hopeless pursuit," replied Shannon.

"It's hopeless for me. Those cards just didn't play out in my favor. I'm just destined to be a hustler like my grandfather. And he did alright for himself," said John.

After ten minutes of talking, they realized it was time to leave Alexis and Tina alone. John heard heavy breathing coming from the hot tub. He turned around and saw their friends making out aggressively.

"I think we need to go," said John.

"That's fine. I need to get home anyway," replied Shannon.

"What about her?" asked John about Tina.

"Do you think Alexis can give her a ride?" asked Shannon.

"One second," said John. He turned around to ask his friend. "Guapos! Can you take Tina home?"

"Sure, no problem," huffed Alexis before continuing to Kiss Tina's neck.

John walked Shannon to her car. Neither wanted the evening to end, but Shannon had to return to her other life. She would take with her a new perspective. One that left her lost in a cloud of doubt and new possibilities.

"I'm really glad we spent time together. I never met anyone like you, John," said Shannon.

"I have to tell you, I feel the same," replied John.

"Wait, I'm not finished," said Shannon before letting out a deep breath. "This is a very confusing time for me.

I mean, there's so much happening in my life right now.

I never expected to meet you, and that kind of scares me."

"Why?" asked John. "Was it something I said?"

"No, not at all. But the last year has kind of been a disaster for me. I finished high school early to get a jumpstart on college. But then my parents' drama got in the way, and I thought I could start over in Florida. And then my boyfriend decided to come with me. I mean, financially, it made sense if he was going to work. But then everything went to shit, and I'm not even in love 'with him. Now, I feel like a married woman who hasn't even finished college. That thought terrifies me, and I don't know what to do."

They both heard huffing and moaning coming from the backyard patio. It was an intense sound that indicated how much Alexis and Tina were enjoying each other's company. As funny as it was to John and Shannon, it added to the awkwardness of their situation. Shannon was torn between a small sense of loyalty to her boyfriend and her immediate attraction to John. The sounds of sex in the air did not make the situation any easier.

"I feel something between us. Something that I've never felt with my boyfriend. And I'm not sure what to do about it. But I shouldn't be here any longer. I'm sorry. I have to go," said Shannon. "I'll see you at work."

She gave John a kiss on the cheek and stepped inside her car. John watched her drive away until she turned a corner to exit the neighborhood. Meanwhile, Alexis and Tina continued to hump like rabbits.

"Harder! Harder! Harder!" yelled Tina.

John smiled before lighting a cigarette. He stayed in the driveway to ponder what Shannon had said. He understood her situation and did not want to add any more grief to the girl's life.

Before the cigarette finished, he reaffirmed to himself that the heist was the top priority. He looked at the stars and imagined a successful score. He didn't understand why it all came to be, but he was certain that they were following destiny.

John arrived home with a heavy mind, hoping to get a good night's sleep. From the parking lot, he noticed the living room light was on, which was unusual considering it was one in the morning. He stepped out of his car and 'walked to the apartment. After opening the door, he saw his mother sprawled across the living room floor.

"Mom!" yelled John. This time, Betsy was the one who tried to commit suicide. There was a spilled bottle of Xanax next to her. John noticed that her skin was pale, and her breathing was faint. He turned her around and tried to slap her awake. After a few light taps, he could not get a response and started to panic.

"Shit! Shit! Shit! Mom, wake up! Onnit Vincent! Where the fuck are you?"

Nobody was home. John was all alone with his dying mother. He knew he needed to act quickly. So, he gently repositioned her head on the floor and used his cell phone to call the paramedics.

"911 emergency, can you provide the address of the

emergency?" asked the dispatcher.

"twenty-two-eleven, Sandpiper lane, Boynton beach, three-three-four-three-seven," said john.

"What's the emergency?" asked the dispatcher.

"My mom, she overdosed on Xanax. I need help... quick. She's dying," he said.

John put down the phone and proceeded to conduct mouth-to-mouth resuscitation without having any formal training. After tilting her head to elevate her chin, he gave three deep breaths into her airway. He began to pump on her chest in hopes of getting any sign of life. After not getting a response, he gave her another three breaths of air and proceeded again to pump on her chest. That was when she coughed, and her eyes opened slightly. They rolled to the back of her head, exposing only the corneas.

"Wake up, Mom! Wake up!"

John held his dying mother in his arms until the paramedics arrived. She was barely alive when they placed her inside the ambulance. He gave the police officer his information and got into his car to go to the hospital.

Before turning on the ignition, he took a minute to assess what he had just seen. It was utter disbelief that nobody else was there and that his mother could die. As 'much as he wanted to, John could not cry. He never cried. Instead, he bottled up his feelings and hid them in a deep abyss of sadness.

'Alexis and Tina were still having sex when John called. He immediately drove Tina home and then headed to JFK medical to be with his buddy. When he finally got there, John was sitting in the waiting room, staring at the ground with both hands clinched like he was praying.

"What's up, bro? Is your mom okay?" asked Alexis.

"Dude, I don't know. I got home, and she was unconscious, like comatose. I had to revive her. The doctors are with her right now," said John.

"Fuck, where the hell is Onni? Does your brother know?" asked Alexis.

"I don't know where the fuck Onni is. I saw him this morning walking around the kitchen, but that's it. And fucking Vincent hasn't picked up his phone," said john 'with panic in his eyes. He was trying his hardest to suppress his emotions.

"Sorry, man... she's going to be fine," said Alexis.

They sat in the waiting room for an hour until the attending physician arrived. It was the same doctor that treated Onni when he overdosed.

"Mr. Thibault, how are you? We've managed to stabilize your mother. She'll be able to go home in a few days at most. The combination of alcohol and benzodiazepines almost killed her. She's really lucky that you arrived home at the time you did. Otherwise, she wouldn't have made it."

"Is there some type of... help... that the hospital can provide. I mean, I really don't know what I'm doing here, and I need help," pleaded John.

"There isn't much else we can do. She obviously needs help. I remember her and you. I had to resuscitate her husband last week. Where is he?" asked Dr. Cardoso.

"I don't know," replied John.

"There's a clinic in Lake Worth that's not as fancy as the other places, but they're honest and good at what they do. It's called Casa de Luz. Look them up if you want. We'll be in touch," said Dr. Cardoso before walking away.

John felt lost. His family was destroyed, and it made him feel like a failure for not keeping everyone together. Despite all the beatings, lies, abandonment, distrust, and 'maniacal rants, part of him still felt they would all be together one day. As juvenile as the idea was, he never accepted that his parents had fallen out of love.

"Hey man, let's go. I'll roll up a blunt to help you sleep," said Alexis.

While sitting in his car, John tried to regain his mental equilibrium before turning on the car's ignition. After a few minutes of just sitting there, Alexis stepped to the passenger side of the car, and John unlocked the door. He sat down and handed John the blunt.

"Calm your nerves, bro. Take a minute to relax your 'mind. Don't think about anything right now. Not even the heist," advised Alexis.

"What? No, fuck that. No, this doesn't change anything. We're stealing the card on New Year's from that museum," said John. He needed the heist because he needed to feel a sense of control over his own life. He also needed a way to better his family's broken situation.

"Are you sure?" asked Alexis before taking a hit.

"We have to plant the cameras in the next couple of days and find out what happens with that card at night. I 'have a feeling that he leaves everything there."

John took a hit of the blunt and continued. "Look, man... you're going to be fine in life. You'll graduate and make a shitload of money someday. Me, this is as good as it gets. And if I'm ever going to move forward in life, we need to steal that baseball card from that fucking museum. My life depends on it. My family depends on it."

Alexis hadn't realized how emotionally invested John was in the heist. To him, it was still nothing but a game. He understood the risks but figured he was too smart to get caught. John, on the other hand, was betting his entire life on the heist.

Chapter Twelve

The next morning, John awoke to a phone call. He scrambled to find it because it had fallen underneath his bed. When he saw that it was his mother, he felt an immense sense of relief.

"Mom, are you okay?" he said.

"Yeah... can you please come?" said Betsy, who sounded weak.

John took a quick shower and returned to the hospital. When he arrived at her room, she was fully awake, sitting in a chair by the window. He was elated to see her alive, but the trauma from the evening held back any sign of that.

"Hi, Mom. How do you feel?" he asked.

Betsy just looked at him and nodded her head. She struggled to speak because of the tube that had been shoved down her throat to pump her stomach. But her eyes never stopped staring at John. The sight of her firstborn son was a powerful reminder of her failure as a mother.

"Johnny, I'm so sorry," she muttered before breaking down in tears. "I'm sorry, and I'll never do this again. You and Vincent deserve better."

"It's okay, Mom. Don't cry. You're a great mom. You always have been," replied John.

"No, I haven't... not for a long time. This isn't the way life was supposed to be, not for my sons," said Betsy.

John sat in a chair next to his mother. He put his hand on top of hers as the tears continued to fall from her face.

"What happened? I just came home and found you on the floor," he said.

"Onni and I got into an argument, and he left. I was so upset that I started to drink. And after a while, I convinced myself that I didn't want to live anymore. So... I took half a bottle of pills. And then I woke up in this room and called you," said Betsy.

"Look, Mom. I'm working on something. It's kind of big. But if all goes well, I'm going to get back everything we lost, I promise," said John.

Betsy could barely comprehend what he was saying. Her mind was stuck in a state of shock. Still, John thought he needed to give her hope. It was the only thing left to hold on to.

John stayed with Betsy until she became tired and fell asleep. At that time, neither Onni nor Vincent arrived to see her. When John left, he called his brother three times without getting an answer. After the third time, he left a stern message while standing in the hospital hallway.

"You're a fucking disgrace. I don't know who you think you are these days, but she's your fucking mother, and you need to come see her. JFK, room two-eleven."

It was not even eight-thirty in the morning, and John was wide-awake. He knew that Tanisha was covering the morning shift in the music section because they were short-handed. So, he decided to go to work to pick up some extra hours.

Once at work, all John could think of was Shannon. She was a light that casts over the darkness, and he desperately needed to be around her energy. He waited patiently for her to arrive that afternoon. He expected that, at some point, she would eventually go to see him. But hours passed, and she never did.

The only person who eventually arrived was Angelica. She craved John's attention more than ever, especially since he was distancing himself. John's natural goodness was a major aphrodisiac to broken girls like Angelica. He didn't advertise his criminal tendencies to the women he dated. They only saw a harmless, soft-spoken, white male with innocent eyes and a soft voice.

"I haven't heard from you in two days. What's going on, John?" she said with desperate eyes while entering the music section.

"What do you mean?" replied John, who was deep in thought behind the register. "You have no idea what the fuck I've been through. I really don't need this right now."

"How would I know if you don't tell me? You don't call me. What am I to think?" replied Angelica.

"Angelica, please, I don't need this right now. My mom OD'd last night. I need to be alone," said John.

It was like she did not hear a single thing John said. Angelica could not stop herself from pushing forward with her insecurities. The lack of understanding was all John needed to completely turn away from her.

"I just need you to tell me one thing...," she said.

"Look, I can't date you right now! I'm sorry, Angelica. I can't give you the attention you need. I'm sorry," said John.

"Sorry? John, I just want to be here for you. And if you only had called or said something, then everything would be okay," replied Angelica. She had no idea that she was digging herself into a deeper hole.

"Can you go? I need to get back to work... I'm done with this," said John before picking up a box of CDs and taking them to the other side of the music section.

Angelica finally understood the message and left the music section, crying. John went back to thinking about Shannon. Eventually, he went to find her during his break. After looking through the store's perimeter, he found her conducting an inventory check in the magazine section.

"Hey... Shannon... how are you?" he asked.

She struggled to look at him and covered the fact by continuing to work. John could sense that her demeanor wasn't the same. He wanted to tell her about everything that had happened with his mother. He was seeking her comfort and support.

"I'm good. Sorry, I've been really busy today," replied Shannon before finally looking at John. She immediately noticed that his eyes looked exhausted. "Are you okay? Did you keep partying all night with Alexis?"

"How did you know that I was up late?" replied John.

"I got a phone call last night. I think you butt-dialed me. But I heard you and Alexis talking about something I wasn't supposed to hear," said Shannon.

"What? What are you talking about?" replied John, confused and concerned.

"Something about breaking into a museum on New Year's Eve... look, whatever you're doing, it's your life. And I don't feel right getting involved. But I'm only going to say this once before I walk away. You're too good of a person to fail in life. And if you think this is your only way to succeed, then I'm here to tell you that you're wrong. You don't need to do this."

John knew that there was nothing left to say. He did not want to deny it and belittle her intelligence. He also did not want her to get involved, but it was too late for that. Her words resonated soundly in his head as she walked away to take a break. She would not provide the comfort he sought, and he knew he needed to internalize his emotions deeper than ever.

The next day, John returned to the sports museum with Alexis to plant the cameras and continue as planned. They waited all morning at the parking lot across the street to see if Herb Bowman had arrived at his museum. But after an hour, the only people who arrived were two employees. It was imperative for the boys to take advantage of that small window.

Before getting out of the car, they discussed where the cameras needed to be placed. As always, the matter had to be discussed over a ganja toke.

"So, we gotta focus two of these cameras on the third floor; one facing the display, and another facing the entire floor, somewhere in the back. I'll position that camera to record the hatch door on the roof. I need to know how far of a drop it is from the roof in case we need to use it as an exit route. One camera on the first floor should face the exit; the other should be placed on the west end so we can have a full view of the entire store."

"Alright, I'll get the ones on the first floor," said John. "But let me get one more rip before we go inside."

"Are you sure that you're ready for this? Doesn't your mom come home today?" asked Alexis.

"Yeah, but I think Onni is going to get her. Those two have a lot of things to talk about," answered John.

"Is she still on suicide watch?" asked Alexis.

"I think so, but after three days, the hospital lets them go. But don't worry, the heist comes first," replied John.

"Sure, man... okay," replied Alexis. He could sense the desperation in John's voice.

"Don't you have anything else to say? Are you still into this?" returned John.

"Fuck yeah, but I'm not letting my emotions get involved. I see a goal, and I'm going to follow the plan to reach it. Let's get this shit done," replied Alexis.

They walked into the store and paid the entrance fee to the male attendant. It was a different attendant than the last time they were there. He gave Alexis the receipt, and the boys went their separate ways.

John immediately walked to the west end of the first floor to plant camera one. At the same time, Alexis surveyed the basketball memorabilia to find something cheap to buy. He searched through the signed, unframed posters because they were not as expensive as the cards or the hockey sticks.

After John planted a second camera near the store's entry, Alexis took the elevator to the third floor. He walked to the Honus

Wagner display, where there was an old Jai-alai cesta hanging across from it. It was surrounded by other Jai-alai memorabilia like elbow pads, jerseys, cintas, and helmets. Alexis stuck a camera inside the cesta to directly record the Honus Wagner display. The Jai-alai display provided enough hiding space to securely position another camera that recorded the roof's hatch door.

Meanwhile, John found a signed Scott Mellanby rookie card that was selling for sixty dollars. He idolized the longtime Panther Captain and took the card to the register to buy it. That was when Herb Bowman walked into the room and immediately recognized him.

"My boy... how are you?" asked Herb. He had a snide look on his face as though already suspecting foul play. As a result, he wanted to intimidate John.

"How are you doing, sir?" replied John.

"I'm fine. Did you find something?" asked Herb.

"Yeah," replied a nervous John. "Scott Mellanby." "Nice, nice, Mellanby," replied Herb with a stern look.

"You're Luke Thibault's son, right? The baseball player." "That's right," said John, who had no idea how he'd been identified. "Do you know my dad?"

Herb just stared at John for a second with a pompous smile and a curled lip. John stared back. He wasn't the biggest person, but he wasn't scared of anyone.

"Yeah, I know your dad, your uncles, and your grandfather. I used to see you play at East Boynton for years. You and, ugh, your buddy, Garcia. I owned the concession stand back then."

"Really?" asked John.

"Oh yeah, I follow all the good ones. You two carried the travel team to the state title two years in a row."

"That's right, those were some good times," replied John. "Excuse me, but..." said John in the hope of cutting the conversation short.

"You know, I didn't realize who you were when I saw you at the show. But after the last time you came here with your Mexican friends, I knew I recognized you. So... how come you've been hanging around here so much?" asked Herb bluntly.

"What? I'm just a customer. That's all. Pm here to make a purchase. But if you want me to leave, I will," said John, who pretended to be insulted.

"No, go ahead, please... proceed with your purchase. And then I want you and Garcia to get out of here. Do you understand?"

That was when Alexis returned to find John and Herb talking. He had finished planting all the cameras and was ready to leave as quickly as possible. But the look on John's face told him it would not go so smoothly.

"I'm telling this to you too, Garcia," said Herb. Alexis was also oblivious to how Herb knew his name. "Don't come back here... either of you."

"Man, fuck this guy. Let's get out of here," said a defiant Alexis. He barged towards the exit, bumping Herb Bowman out of the way with his broad shoulder. Herb fell back on a souvenir display, knocking down some cups and picture frames.

"Get the fuck out of my way," added Alexis before he and John walked out the door.

John felt the plan was ruined. His heart was racing as they walked to the car. But he looked over at Alexis, who had a prideful, gangster look on his face.

"That was not cool. You shouldn't have done anything," said John.

"Fuck that old motherfucker. He's just paranoid. He doesn't have a clue about what we're doing. And how the fuck does he know my name?" said Alexis before stepping into the car.

"He says he remembers us from baseball. He knew that we were on the same team and had won the state titles. He also said he knows my family. He said he knew my dad, my uncles, and my grandpa. The funny thing is that I saw his stupid commercial on TV the other day with my dad, and he mentioned the guy had legal problems with my grandfather back in the day," said John.

"Fuck, and now we're not allowed back in there. I have to get back inside to retrieve the cameras. If not, I can't pull the SD cards and review the recordings," said Alexis while driving. That was when Alexis's mind went into survival mode. He quickly thought of a solution, one that he did not like but felt was necessary.

"We can use Brian," he said while focusing on the road. "I can tell him where they are, and he can go get it. He never played sports. So, this guy doesn't know who he is."

"Dude, I don't know if I like that idea," said John.

"What? Why? I can't think of anything else," replied Alexis.

"You know why. He's fucking Brian! He's pretty much the shadiest person I have ever met in my life. Not to mention he was like... your best friend and fucked your girlfriend behind your back," expressed John.

"Hey, man! Why the fuck you gotta bring that up!?" said Alexis.

"Cause I'm your bro, and I'm trying to make a point. Chill out," said John before rolling down the window and lighting a cigarette."

Alexis understood John's point. He knew Brian could not be trusted, not when there was money involved. In a fight, certainly. But to pull a heist, his reliance was questionable. After three years, he was still uncomfortable with the topic of Brian's betrayal.

"I hear you, John. But at this point, we gotta do it. That high school shit is in the past. He's gotta get those cameras for us. And either he'll choose to make amends for what happened, or he'll fuck us over. And if he does, I'll find a way to put that motherfucker to sleep," said Alexis as he drifted away in vengeful thought. "I'll put that motherfucker to sleep."

"What about the buyer? Have you contacted anyone?" asked John.

"Yeah, Leo's setting me up with his dealer. The guy is coming back from Oregon to see his kids. Apparently, he knows someone that might want to buy the card. I've met him before. He seems decent. The only thing is, he'll probably ask for a cut," said Alexis.

"How much do you think is enough?" asked John.

"We'll give him three thousand and Brian ten thousand. I figured that we could sell the card for 1.6 million," said Alexis.

"One-point-six? Why not two?" asked John.

"Because we need to hawk it, fast, and at rock bottom price. Remember, we gotta get rid of this thing before the world gets word that it's been stolen. Otherwise, the buyer will know where it came from," replied Alexis.

The next day, John returned to work with a sharp focus. Shannon was around, but they never spoke. In his mind, whatever was or was not happening with her would have to wait. He did not have the emotional tolerance to think of her, or his mom, his dad, his brother, and definitely not Onni.

For a good while, it seemed the day would pass quickly. But then he heard commotion coming from the book floor. He looked over the bookshelf and confirmed a man's voice screaming by the store's entrance.

"What do you want from me!?"

The threatening tone forced John to leave his post and check on Shannon. He ran to the front and saw a young man in a tantrum, kicking over a café table. There was rage in his eyes. Other customers felt threatened and moved out of the crazy man's way. Then he saw Shannon standing across from him with a concerned look on her face.

"Do you actually think you can leave me?" said the young man to Shannon.

"You need to go. You're acting like a fool," she replied.

The young man with short, dark hair was Shannon's boyfriend. He stormed out the door to the parking lot, and Shannon followed. All the other customers and workers aimed their attention toward the drama occurring outside the store.

Shannon stayed close to the building, watching her boyfriend march across the parking lot. He unlocked the trunk of his car and took out a baseball bat. From there, he jumped on the hood of Shannon's car and yelled at her in dramatic fashion.

"If you want me to leave? Then I'm giving you something to remember me by!"

"David, you're being ridiculous. Stop!" said Shannon.

Infuriated, David lifted the bat over his head and pounded it on the hood multiple times. Shannon watched in sadness, slowly accepting the reality that her relationship was over. John walked outside to support her and asked, "Are you okay? Is that your boyfriend?"

"I told him last night that... I didn't want to be in a relationship anymore. And he won't accept it," said Shannon, who was distraught but relieved to see him.

"Don't worry… the cops are on the way. You can stay at my place if you want. I mean... if you're okay with that," said John.

David stepped down from the car and noticed John. He became engulfed with vengeful fury at the sight of another man comforting his girlfriend.

"Hey! Get the fuck away from her," said David with his chest pumped and full of air. He started walking towards John and Shannon with the bat still in hand.

"You better get the fuck out of here," said John after stepping in front of Shannon to protect her. But before David could cross the road, the police arrived. Two patrol cars stopped in front of the store, and the officers jumped out with their guns drawn.

"Sir! Put down the weapon and put your hands in the air!" said one of the officers with war tats on his right arm.

David quickly snapped back into reality and did as the officers commanded. He dropped to his knees, put the bat on the ground, and lay face-down on the street. The cops moved forward with guns drawn and put him in handcuffs. John and Shannon watched as the police put him in the back of a squad car and drove away. Meanwhile, Angelica took a long look at John with his arm around Shannon and then ran out of the cafeteria crying.

Chapter Thirteen

Joel Martinez was Leo's weed supplier who was living in Eugene, Oregon. He grew up in Puerto Rico but moved to Florida when he was fifteen. His father built a respectable tree service company in Boynton Beach, providing Joel with opportunities to run up the electrical and water bill when growing pot.

Before moving away to Oregon, he grew weed behind the tree nursery and sold bulk quantities to Leo, who distributed it all over the county. The business venture brought them both a substantial profit, but it eventually put Joel's father's business at risk. So, Joel distanced himself from the family business and moved to the Pacific to become a cultivator.

Three days after moving away, the local police raided the tree nursery. But they found nothing. Other than the minor inconvenience it caused his father, Joel slipped by the local law enforcement and fled westward like a bandit.

For Leo, that marked the start of a brief absence from the weed game. While Joel settled out west, Leo was left to deal skimped eighths and half-eighths for hardly any returns. It was not until the next harvest season that the two finally communicated. Joel ended up shipping Leo forest-grown weed in UPS packages, introducing a better-quality strain to South Florida.

Joel would package the weed, usually a pound at a time, and pay an illegal alien to ship it at the local UPS store. He would send it to one of many P.O. boxes that Leo had set up around South Florida, some in Dade County, some in Broward County, and some in Palm Beach County. Some were even set up as far down south as Key Largo.

That created a system that was difficult for police to monitor. Leo would sell it and then give Joel's cut to his stripper girlfriend, who still lived in Boynton. They were able to sustain the distribution ring for over a year without any difficulties. That was how Leo was able to fund the Honus Wagner heist.

A few days after planting the cameras, Leo drove Alexis to the Royal Palm Acreage to meet Joel at his father's new tree nursery. He spent the entire ride explaining to Alexis how they were moving weed across the country. He also updated Alexis on Joel's adopted family situation.

"So, he's still with that stripper chick?" asked Alexis while sitting in the passenger seat of Leo's truck.

"Yup, and she's still dancing around with other dudes. But it's the kid... Joel loves him to death," replied Leo.

"He's too nice. It would be hard to raise a child that wasn't mine, especially if the mom is fucking around with other guys she meets at work," said Alexis.

When they arrived at the nursery, Joel was attending to a female customer who was interested in six chrysanthemum plants. Leo and Alexis got out of the truck and strolled the lot as if they were common customers. Alexis admired all of the plant species, including palms, ferns, shrubs, magnolias, mangroves, and fruit trees.

"Thank you so much... and remember about your cats, they're attracted to these plants. If they eat off it, they'll get sick," advised Joel to the customer before she walked away.

"Sandro, ayúdale a la señora, por favor," said Joel to one of his workers.

Joel walked over to the palms display where Leo and Alexis were waiting. He was covered in dirt from an honest day's work.

"What's up, dude?" said Joel to Leo before they slapped hands. "How'd you like that last pound I sent you?"

"Fucking fire. This guy said he wanted to fuck it," replied Leo while pointing to Alexis.

"What's up with you, bud?" said Joel, who was amused by the banter.

"Not much, bro. How's Oregon? I heard it's like the Wild West over there," said Alexis.

"Pretty much. I mean, there's a lot of room to work. A lot of people out there growing in the mountains. It's not an easy place for the DEA to investigate, but they pop up from time to time. My partner and I had to move the operation twice just to make sure we weren't next," explained Joel. "So, what's up? How can I help you?"

They took a stroll through the nursery to maintain privacy. It was the perfect setting to discuss a two-million-dollar heist. Alexis knew that he could be direct with Joel and expected a direct answer in return.

Although he was a drug dealer, Joel was not violent. His mild-mannered nature was always appreciated by all of his business partners.

"So, look, I got a rare baseball card. It's worth two million dollars. I need to find a buyer for it. And I need that buyer to meet with me on January 1st before sunrise," said Alexis as his brother listened.

"Two million dollars? Where the fuck... you know what, never mind," replied Joel, who couldn't help from chuckling.

"Yeah, that's the thing. I can't reveal how I *got* it. I just *want* to get rid of it fast at a lowball price," said Alexis.

"That's pretty much what your brother said," replied Joel while looking at Leo.

"I told you," added Leo.

"I actually know someone who might be interested. Apart from his various business interests, this dude is a collector. And I don't recommend trying to cross him. That's probably the best advice I can give you about dealing with this guy. I actually mentioned everything to him after your brother said you were in the market for a buyer. He's here to talk," revealed Joel.

"Aww, dude, this is kind of a surprise," said Leo, who was caught off guard.

"What are you talking about, Leo? I told you he was coming," replied Joel.

"You did?" asked Leo.

"Yes! As soon as you called me, I told you that I'd give him a call to come by in a few days... You gotta stop smoking so much, brother," said Joel.

"Oh yeah, now I remember, I think," replied Leo.

Alexis rolled his eyes in response to his brother's sloppiness. But he wasn't bothered or surprised. In fact, it appealed to him to get the matter handled as soon as possible. He considered it as progress.

"So, where is he?" asked Alexis.

"Back here, over by the chickens," said Joel.

"Aww, dude, you're going to love this. His dad raises fighting roosters," mentioned Leo to his little brother.

They walked to the farthest corner of the nursery, where seven roosters were being held in cages. There was also an area dedicated to training. At the far end of the area, a young man in his thirties was admiring a large, white-feathered rooster. He had a short, buzzed haircut, wore jeans and a t-shirt, and looked harmless.

"Oh shit, this one's really pissed," he said in a British accent while observing the fighting chicken.

"William, this is Alexis and Leo. They're the brothers I told you about," said Joel.

"How are you, boys?" said William. "Joel here tells me that you have a rare baseball card. May I ask who it is?"

Alexis paused a few seconds before engaging in the negotiation. He understood that William was looking for all the details upfront, which he appreciated. But he also needed to protect his own interests at the same time.

"So, let's say we're telling the truth... and I have a highly valuable card to sell you. How does this work?" asked Alexis.

"Well, if you want it all on the table... we would choose a meeting point, just as long as the price is right. We'll gladly buy the card from you... in cash, and walk away," said William.

"I like that; the quicker, the better," replied Alexis. "We can meet wherever you say. We'll be using a boat, so anywhere near the ocean is preferred.

"So, where are you thinking?" replied William.

"Maybe the Keys or Bahamas," suggested Alexis.

"It's funny you say that. My boss is actually the one interested in the card. I'm just the messenger. But he has a house on Lucaya Beach, on the south end of the island. Could we meet there?" asked William.

"I don't see why not," replied Alexis.

"Okay, but I need more details about the card," iterated William.

Alexis and Leo looked at each other for a second to see how the other felt about giving that information. The smooth, quick dialogue provided a comfortable negotiation experience, but Alexis was hesitant to reveal the card's identity for fear of jeopardizing the heist. But William wanted to assure the Garcia brothers that he was only interested in an honest business transaction.

"Look," said William. "Whatever fucking business we're doing here, it's illegal, no matter how you spin it. If this card is worth as much as you say it is, and it's not being sold under the supervision of a regulatory agency, then it's all... against... the law. Fuck, if you're worrying about me stealing it, don't. I only negotiate. We prefer to leave the dirty work to the laborers."

"It's the T206 Honus Wagner card. And I'm selling it for one-point-five million. I can deliver it to your boss's house on January 1st. Talk to him, and let us know," said Alexis.

"Right on, I'll deliver the message. We'll be in contact,"

replied William to end the conversation.

He walked away for a few steps before turning around and saying, "Send me a list of all the equipment you'll need. Joel will give you my number."

Chapter Fourteen

John was smoking a bowl on his bed. He was watching a Stanley Kubrick film, trying to relax from the anxiety of not having heard from Alexis about the buyer situation. He'd settled into a personal mindset, focusing on nothing but the heist.

He heard a knock at the window, expecting it to be Alexis. But when he opened the curtain, he was surprised to see Shannon standing there instead. She was holding a book bag full of items. Without hesitating, John instructed her to go to the front door.

"Just in time," said John to welcome her. "My mom's asleep, so let's just go to the room."

"Oh, okay. Do you want me to take off my shoes?" she asked in a low tone while walking inside the apartment. "I mean, if you don't mind," replied John.

"No, not at all," said Shannon before taking off her flats.

John grabbed Shannon's bag, and they walked to the room without making noise. He put her belongings on the couch and said, "Here, take a seat, relax. Do you want anything to drink or eat?"

"Um, no thanks. I'm fine. Sorry, I arrived later than I'd planned, but I went back to the apartment to grab a few things."

"It's alright. I wasn't sure if you were coming. But I'm glad you did... So, where's your ex?" asked John.

"Um, I'm not sure. He might still be in jail. I haven't heard anything since the cops took him away."

"Do you want something to drink? A coffee?" asked John.

"Sure, that'll work," replied Shannon.

John left the room, and she started to observe the furniture and the fixtures on his wall. Every piece of furniture was made of fine oak. She thought it made the apartment bedroom look smaller. She also paid attention to the well-rounded collection of sports memorabilia on his wall. He had twelve signed plaques organized in a sixty-two arrangement. Shannon had no idea who any of the athletes were, nor did she care.

Next to the dresser, John had an old wooden barrel on display. And next to the door was the largest collection of DVD movies that she had ever seen on a large rack. Again, it seemed that they were all organized in a manner specific to John's liking. There were westerns, every Rocky movie, fantasy, thrillers, and classics from the eighties.

He opened the door as Shannon was staring at the baseball team picture. First, she noticed John, and then she noticed Alexis, who was sitting next to John.

"You're so cute in this picture... so young. Is that your friend, Alexis?" she asked while taking a closer look.

"Yep, we were pretty good back then," replied John.

Shannon read the players' and coaches' names on the picture. When she got to the end, she noticed that the coach had John's last name, *Coach Luke Thibault.*

"Is that your dad?" she asked.

"Yep, that was the last year that he coached," said John.

He no longer wanted to talk about the photo. Instead, he pressed 'play' on the DVD player and threw himself on the bed. Shannon was not sure how to feel at that moment. Although her long-term relationship had just ended, John had her attention in every way imaginable.

"I'm so exhausted. Do you mind if I lie on the bed with you?" she asked.

"No, not at all," said John before moving against the wall. "Sorry, it's only a twin."

"It's fine. It's just nice to get off my feet. I really appreciate you letting me stay here, John," replied Shannon.

She curled up against him as they watched the film. Out of respect, he battled every impulse in his mind to refrain from making a move. And after twenty minutes, exhaustion prevailed. With the movie still playing, John and Shannon fell asleep in an innocent embrace.

Shannon was awakened by the early sunlight. For a moment, she forgot where she was. And then John, who was still in a deep state of sleep, grunted. She turned around to look at him and acknowledge the peace she felt.

Shannon stepped out of bed, grabbed her bag, and went to the bathroom to get dressed. After finishing, she walked out of the bathroom and ran into Vincent, who was just getting home. She noticed him wearing a championship wrestling belt around his waist and found it to be a bit awkward.

"Hey," he said. "I'm John's brother."

"Hi, I'm Shannon... we were hanging out, and I fell asleep," said Shannon, who didn't want to appear like a late-night fling.

"Do you need anything? Some coffee?" asked Vincent, who was humored to find a girl entering his brother's room at seven in the morning.

"No, I'm fine. I'm just... off to work," she replied. "Okay, nice meeting you," said Vincent before going to his room.

Shannon returned to the room and found John sitting on the edge of his bed, still trying to awaken his senses.

He looked up at her, and she said, "I met your brother. He went to his room."

"Vincent? Is he here? I'm surprised," said a groggy John. "Oh, he doesn't live here?" asked Shannon.

"Yeah, but he's never home. That kid lives in his own world," replied John.

Shannon was not about to conduct an interview about the matter. She did not want to seem nosey. So, she just nodded her head to end the conversation about Vincent.

"I have to go open the store today," she said after sitting on the bed next to John.

"You can stay as long as you need. I'm serious. It's not a problem," said John.

"Thanks, John. I really appreciate everything. But I need to go face the music. I'm not sure if he's there or not, but there needs to be closure," replied Shannon.

"Okay, but if you need anything, let me know," he replied.

She leaned forward and kissed John on the lips, galvanizing his soul. In a single act, Shannon helped shed away his crippling worries. Their connection didn't feel like an infatuation, not to either one. It felt like something meaningful.

Shannon left John in a blissful trance. After seeing her pull out of the parking lot through his bedroom window, he looked at his phone to check the time. It was eight in the morning, and there was a text message from Alexis. It read: *Class was canceled. Meeting with Brian to talk about the cameras at Ocean Cafe.*

Over by the train tracks, Alexis and Brian were fogging out the inside of Alexis's Pontiac. For Alexis, it felt awkward seeing Brian consecutive times. He thought they would never again hang like that. But life being what it is, some friendships will always find a way to reunite.

"So, what happened to Joe? Franky? You guys aren't kicking anymore?" asked Alexis.

The question jolted a unique reaction in Brian. He stared deep out the windshield and replied, "Na... no, man, I stopped talking to those guys a while ago."

"Really? I thought you all made a lot of money selling weed up there in Jacksonville," said Alexis."

Just then, the back door opened, and John stepped into the car. The unexpected entrance jolted both Brian and Alexis' nervous systems. For a second, they both thought they were getting arrested or robbed.

"Whoa, someone's having a party here said John after sitting in the car.

"What's up, *man!?*" said Brian.

"What's up, Brian!? Good to see you, bro," said John. "How's Jacksonville?"

"Fucking amazing. I don't know what you two guys are still doing here," replied Brian.

Alexis passed the blunt to John, who immediately took five hits in succession.

"So, what happened to Joe and Franky?" continued Alexis.

"Bro, those two guys set me up and took a lot of my money. We don't talk anymore," said Brian.

"Bitch-ass-Joe stole from you?" asked John. "That's funny. He cried in the ninth grade because somebody stole his watch. Now he's robbing people?"

"We were making so much money, selling weed and pills to the entire campus. Then this one day, I was supposed to drop off one-hundred-and-fifty thousand dollars to this guy who was going to get me some ecstasy. On the way there, two guys walked up to me at a gas station and robbed me at gunpoint. I immediately felt like it was some type of setup, and those two were the only ones who knew about it. So, I called them to see what was up, but neither picked up their phone. Joe transferred to school somewhere down here, and Franky disappeared off the face of the planet."

"Oh shit, were they the ones who physically robbed you?" asked John.

"No, it was two other white guys. But I think Franky and Joe hired someone to do it. It all led to bigger problems that almost got me killed. So, I said, 'fuck it.' I came back here to stay with my parents for the holidays, but it might be permanent. So, whatever you guys need me to do, I'm good for it." said Brian.

Alexis looked at John through the rearview minor. They were thinking the same thing. To them, it sounded like Brian was in a desperate situation. They weren't sure how literal Brian was about his offer. But they were about to find out.

"We need you to go inside the museum and retrieve the cameras we planted. There are four in total, two on the third floor and two on the first floor. We've already been flagged by the owner of the place, and I shoved him when he got tough with us the other day. So, we can't go back there. We just need you to walk in, browse, and get the cameras. I'll tell you exactly where they are so you can do it quickly... What do you think?" said Alexis.

"You know exactly where they are?" asked Brian. "Yeah, they're hidden. But if we tell you the spot, you shouldn't have a problem finding them," said John.

"So, what's my cut going to be? For the boat and getting the cameras?" asked Brian without hesitation.

Again, Alexis looked at John to get a read on his reaction. And then he answered with a random number, far greater than they originally planned to give him.

"Twenty thousand...;' blurted Alexis.

"Okay, that's a good number. I'll do it," replied Brian.

John and Alexis were taken aback by the easiness of the negotiation. They were expecting Brian to haggle to some degree. Up until that point, the heist was seemingly falling into place.

"Alright, bro. Can you go today?" asked Alexis.

Brian just nodded his head and curled down his bottom lip to say, *'sure, no problem.'*

"Alright, let's go inside, get some breakfast, and we'll tell you where everything is," said Alexis.

They entered the café high as kites. The three delinquents chose a table and sat in the chairs. It felt as though they were back in high school, a time when blind trust existed among friends. Although those days were gone, they were still missed by everybody there.

When the food arrived, Brian was the first to dig in with his fork. But before putting the pancake in his mouth, he paused to talk about an old memory.

"I was driving on Military the other day in Boca. And I passed the neighborhood where you got in that fight, Alexis."

"What fight? Where was this?" replied Alexis.

"In the cul-de-sac, that party, in Delaire," said Brian. "Oh yeah, how could I forget?" said Alexis.

"Oh man, that night was insane added John.

"I hate to think about that night because it's the only fight I ever lost," said Alexis.

"You didn't lose that fight. You were working that guy for a long time. And then he grabbed hold of you and wrestled you to the ground," said John.

Alexis allowed his mind to go back to that evening. It was a defining moment in his life. He and Leo showed all the schools in Boca Raton, public and private, who the Garcia brothers were and how well they could fight.

"That party got out of control. Every school in Boca and Delray was there. Those public school kids showed up looking for a fight," said John.

"That fucking asshole shouldn't have hit my beer out of my hands. I don't care how drunk I was or how big he was. That was a dickhead move."

"All I remember was seeing you and that marine squaring up in the middle of that cul-de-sac. A bunch of people wanted to jump in, but others kept saying, 'one on one, one on one.' And then, out of nowhere, Leo's fighting off like five dudes. I turn around, and he's just slamming people against the cars... and when that guy had you pinned, I just remember Brian nailing him with an uppercut."

"Well, it's nice to hear someone say that I held my own. 'That fucking marine was too old to be at that party. Didn't he kill that kid from Lake Worth Christian a few months later?" said Alexis.

"That's right. He and his friends stomped that dude to death at that other party on the water. What a crazy time that was," replied Brian.

"Yeah, the next day, I got a bunch of phone calls. People thought I was the one who got killed."

For the rest of the meal, Alexis, John, and Brian discussed the details of the camera's location. Brian could no longer be trusted. He ruined that with a single act of betrayal. But on this occasion, John and Alexis had no other choice but to make an exception. Trusting Brian to any degree would be the riskiest part of the entire heist. If it were not for saving him the night of that fight, there would be no reason for Alexis to ever trust him again.

Chapter Fifteen

CHRISTMAS EVE, 2001

John, Alexis, and Leo were all standing on a dock at the Arthur Marshall Wildlife Refuge. The area was part of the Florida Everglades Reserve, isolated out west from the rest of suburbia. The refuge stretched nearly the entire western border of Palm Beach County, south to Coral Springs and north to Southern boulevard. The main entrance to the park was in Delray, off State Road 7.

From where they stood, the western horizon of the Everglades was formed by endless miles of sawgrass. There were multiple controlled fires in the distance, disbursing thick clouds of smoke into the sky. Down by the sweet water, the boys marveled at the sight of three monstrous alligators lurking around the dock.

"This big boy is hungry," said John as he followed the giant gator with his eyes.

"Where the fuck is Brian? Are you sure he's coming?" complained Leo.

"I mean, unless he got arrested, he should be coming straight from the museum," said Alexis.

"Oh, fat boy hungry. Must get to the fiesta to have mama's cooking," badgered John to lighten the mood. But he was also doubting if Brian was going to arrive. Their little reunion did nothing to change his mind. To him, Brian was still a dirty scoundrel who could never be trusted. He liked the kid, but only as an acquaintance.

"So, what are you doing tomorrow? Christmas at your mom's?" Alexis asked John.

"No, my grandparent's place. Gotta have dinner with the Don. My dad, his brothers, and all the cousins will be there," replied John.

"What about your mom? What's she gonna do?" continued Alexis.

"She'll probably just stay home. Onni's there, so they'll just keep each other company," said John.

Five minutes later, they saw truck lights down the road. It was heading their way through the bush. There was nobody else at the park, so the truck's appearance put them on alert.

"I think that's him," said Alexis.

The white truck pulled into a parking space aggressively. The door opened, blazing hardcore music into the air. Brian stepped out of the truck with a book bag around his shoulder. He remained stone-faced, giving little indication as to whether he was successful in retrieving the cameras.

"What's up, man? How'd it go?" asked an anxious Alexis.

"Man, that fucking guy was there, the owner. He was eyeballing me the entire time," said Brian.

"Did he tell you anything?" asked John.

"No, but he wanted to. Every time I went to one of the spots, he would walk by to see what I was doing. So, I had to be quick," explained Brian.

He took the four cameras out of his bag and handed them to

Alexis.

"I put the cameras in my pocket, and he started to follow me outside. But I just got in my car and dipped," said Brian.

"That motherfucker," said Alexis.

John, Alexis, and Leo all looked at the cameras and then looked at Brian. They were somewhat in disbelief. Brian had done something that was extremely important to their success. Additionally, he proved their doubt wrong.

"Damn, Brian, you did good. I guess we just need to check these things out and see if the coast is clear," said Alexis.

"When are we going to do that?" asked John.

"I'll let you know what I find in a couple of days. After that, we can start running through the plan," said Alexis.

Later that evening, while his family embarked on the yearly Christmas festivities, Alexis stayed in his room to review the footage. He removed the SD card from the camera and inserted it inside a Sony camcorder. As the sound of his father's drunk rants filled the hallways, Alexis sat on the edge of his bed with the lights off to get a better view of the footage. The only light in the room came from the camera screen.

Alexis arranged to view each SD card based on the assigned order. SD card one was for camera one, which gave a view of the entire museum starting from its west wing. At first glance, he was surprised to see how clear the footage was. He fast-forwarded the video to the evening hours and zoomed to the third floor. At no point did he see Herb Bowman approach the display before closing hours.

Camera two also gave a wide view of the entire store from the south side by the entrance. Again, Alexis fast-forwarded to the closing hours. He saw Herb Bowman carry some items to his office on the third floor and then saw him close out the register. He reviewed the process for the three days the camera recorded and came to a soft conclusion. Mr. Bowman left everything intact after closing the store. That angle also gave a view of the hatch door on the roof. It became clear to Alexis that nobody ever tampered with or even paid attention to the roof entrance.

The third camera was from the Jai-alai cesta. It recorded direct footage of the Honus Wagner display. That view made Alexis realize that the display was undeniably the museum's central attraction. Within three days, he saw about fifty people gather at the display. There were grandfathers, fathers, sons, and daughters who made their way to the museum to view the coveted piece of baseball history. But most importantly, that camera confirmed that Herb Bowman never minded the card. It remained on its display for three days without ever being opened or moved.

Lastly, Alexis viewed camera four which gave a better view of the roof's hatched door. From that view, Noah could measure the drop's distance and observe the door's details at a closer view. He could not believe how simple everything was unfolding.

Then, out of nowhere, Alexis heard a revolting burp. He turned around and saw Leo standing at the doorway of his room with a bottle of gin in his hand.

"Why the fuck are you up here?" he said in an impatient tone.

"Bro, this guy just leaves the card there. He doesn't touch it at all. I saw all the cameras for three days, and he never even got close to them. One of the cameras shows him setting the alarm system. I think that's his only security," replied Alexis.

Over on the island of Palm Beach, the Thibault family gathered at the grandfather's millionaire condo. Things were always tense when the family got together. John's father and uncles all had enormous egos and often held greedy vendettas against each other. Some degree of drama was always imminent.

Thibault Christmas reunions almost always started out the same way, with a lot of alcohol and a lot of food. At first, everyone got along, for grandma's sake. But after three or four whiskeys, the demons started to emerge.

Back in the Christmas of ninety-four, John's uncle, Owen, tried to kill himself in front of the entire family after a long battle with depression. He jumped off the balcony, but Luke grabbed him at the last minute. In ninety-seven, Luke got into a fight with the other brother, Michael, who claimed that Luke had stolen twenty thousand dollars from the corporation.

And one year to the day, Jean Luke kicked Luke out of the family business during Christmas dinner. It was the final straw for ten years of negligence and irresponsibility. Father discovered that his son was using cocaine and showing up drunk to work meetings, and he could not allow it to poison his business.

John invited Shannon to the family dinner. She was alone and unable to return to New Jersey to see her own family for the holidays. To Shannon, it was a comforting and thoughtful gesture. She felt safe with John, no matter how many times he warned her about his family's unpredictable behavior.

They arrived at the beachfront building and took the elevator to the penthouse. His grandmother, Joyce Thibault, opened the door and was elated to see her favorite grandchild and his guest. As always, the Queen of the Thibault family was wearing the latest Palm Beach fashion and jewelry.

"Hello, my dear, I've missed you," said Grandmother Joyce while embracing John and giving him a kiss on the cheek.

"Hi, grandma, I missed you too. This is my friend, Shannon," replied John.

"Oh, hello, Shannon. So nice to meet you. Welcome," replied sweet Grandmother Joyce.

"Thank you so much. You have a beautiful home," replied Shannon, who could see the Atlantic Ocean from the dining room windows.

Luke was sitting on the couch with a drink in his hand. By the look on his face, John could tell that his father was already drunk. It made him nervous that something would happen in front of Shannon.

"Hi, Dad, this is Shannon. She's a friend of mine," said John to his father.

"Hey, Shannon. Glad to see you with my boy," replied Luke as he shook her hand.

Shannon wasn't sure how to react. Based on John's description of the man, he was a maniac. She just smiled humbly, shook his hand, and let the moment pass.

Soon after, John's grandfather, Jean Luke Thibault, walked out of the kitchen with a typical cold look on his face. He was a genius entrepreneur, a hard conservative, and a ruler of the Thibault Empire. For over forty years, he rose among the South Florida business community with a strict dedication to his craft. Except now, he was frail and ill.

"Hey, grandpa, how are you?" said John before cautiously putting his hand on Jean Luke's shoulder.

"I'm fine, John. Good to see you, son," replied Jean Luke as he put his hand on his first-born grandson's shoulder. "And who is this lovely girl?"

"This is Shannon. She's a friend I invited to have dinner with us," explained John.

"Welcome, my darling. Please make yourself at home. Excuse me, I'll be right back," said Jean Luke before leaving back to his room to lie down. He was sick from liver and kidney disease and often rested. He also could not stand the sight of Luke and preferred to be away from him.

John walked to the lavish bar in the middle of the living room to grab a beer and a drink for Shannon. He returned to the couch and handed Shannon a club soda. They sat down to accompany Luke, who was wondering why his father didn't want to talk to him.

"So, what's up, Dad?" said John.

"Not much, not much. How's your mother?" asked Luke while looking at Shannon with his beady eyes. He attempted his best to present a respectable front. But behind those eyes was a scared boy who never grew up. And he was on the brink of a mental meltdown.

"She's getting better. She wasn't feeling too great tonight, so she stayed home," replied John.

Luke abruptly slammed his drink on the coffee table and stood up to pour himself another. John became concerned that Shannon was startled.

"Make sure you take care of her, son... excuse me," said Luke before stumbling to the bar.

John thought it was too early for his father to be plastered. He almost did not want to stay there and was considering leaving. But before that could happen, the rest of the Thibault family arrived.

First came Owen with his wife and two sons. Owen had cleaned up after the suicide attempt. But he continually stole money from the corporation to finance his lavish life. Regardless, he was Jean Luke's baby who always had a soft spot in his father's heart. Jean Luke always gave Owen more leniency than his older brothers.

Instead of going to the door to welcome his brother, Luke stood outside at the balcony bar. His insecurities and pride led him to distance himself from everyone. He no longer knew how to communicate with his own family.

"Hey, brother! Long time no see. Where the hell have you been?" said Owen as he walked onto the balcony.

"Owen! Good to see you, brother," replied Luke as his nephews ran onto the balcony.

"Hi, Uncle Luke!" said one nephew.

"Hi, Uncle Luke!" said the other.

"What have you been doing?" asked Owen.

"I've been managing a couple of places. And I'm trying to

open up a restaurant in Jupiter," replied Luke.

"Oh yeah, Michael mentioned that. He told me you were trying to find the capital to match your partner," replied Owen.

"Yeah, I just need a little to get everything started ...," said Luke before Michael entered through the door with his son and daughter. Michael, like Luke, was also divorced.

"Hey, everybody!" said Michael aloud. He was the leader of the brothers, the responsible one who ran all the family restaurants. He was a lot like his father when it came to the way he conducted business, hardnosed and brutally honest.

Suddenly, Jean Luke reappeared from his room to greet his eldest son. He greeted both his sons, Michael and Owen, and did not mind Luke.

John spent most of the evening on the balcony with Shannon. They sat at a table that was somewhat separated from everyone else. From time to time, he would go back inside to grab a drink or some finger foods. But entertaining Shannon was his priority, and he did not want to overexpose his family to her.

"So, how's everything been at home?" asked John as he handed Shannon a soda.

"Not too bad. He came by and got some things, but I was at work. He left a note saying that he was going to stay with a friend, and that's it," said Shannon.

"That's not so bad. Maybe I can stay over one night,' said John to be fresh.

"I don't know. I really don't want to see Angelica pop up outside my window," replied Shannon to lighten the mood.

"I don't think that's going to happen. It's not like we were ever a couple. I think she's finally starting to accept that," said John, who was craving a cigarette and twitching his leg. But he refrained from smoking to not ruin the moment.

Shannon stared at the ocean to absorb its beauty. The water was choppy. The waves broke near the shoreline, sending dense ocean spray into the air. She thought it was a comfortable setting to ask about the heist. It was less than a week away, and Shannon was terrified that something bad could happen to John. It took every ounce of her courage to bring up the topic, but she knew it was necessary.

"So, what's going on with whatever it is you're doing with Alexis?" she said.

"Huh? What do you mean?" replied John to play dumb. That was when he finally pulled out his box of cigarettes.

"You know what I'm talking about. I'm sorry to bring it up again, but I'm just worried?" said Shannon.

John struggled to conjure his words. He made the mistake of accidentally dialing her, and now he needed to come up with a proper explanation. Normally, he would not care to explain himself. He would have probably left the girl for being too nosey. But Shannon was different, and he knew he owed her the truth.

"I really wish that you didn't hear that. I don't want you to think that I'm some type of sociopath," said John while looking out towards the ocean. "All I can say is, I've been in survival mode for the last five years. I have an opportunity to make some real money and help out my family. And I'm going to do it. I'll understand if you never want to speak to me again, but this is something that I can't pass up."

Shannon did not want to intensify the mood. Although she did not understand why John was willing to risk his life for money, she admired his honesty. Before she could reply, Vincent opened the sliding door with a tune.

"Joy to the world! The Panthers won! ..." chanted Vincent to grab his brother's attention.

John stood up and gave Vincent a hug. It was the only time of the year that they ever embraced. No matter how disappointed John was with his brother, he could never be mad at him.

"Sup, bro, merry Christmas," said John before presenting Shannon. "Uh, I think you two met."

"Hey! I remember you. Merry Christmas," said Vincent before giving Shannon a friendly hug. He then turned to John and gave an unfavorable revelation.

"I just came from the apartment. Mom and Onni were drinking."

"They were?" said John.

"Yeah. I left without saying anything," said Vincent.

By the time dinner started, everybody was drunk. Behind the proper etiquette and the ingenuine smiles, dark thoughts were emerging. John sat between Luke and Shannon. She sat next to Vincent. John's grandparents sat at the head of the table, and his uncles sat across from him.

Joyce's Jamaican maid walked through the kitchen door holding a large platter of meats that included ribeye and salmon.

Bottles of the finest French wine extended from one end of the table to the other. The feast commenced, and the uncles lunged for their meat like ravenous hyenas. All the while, John and Shannon waited patiently to see if any scraps were left behind.

"So, Sharon, how did you two meet?" slurred Luke while chewing his food. John knew better than to correct his father. But out of respect for her, he made the mistake of doing so.

"It's Shannon, Dad," he said to his father.

"What?" replied Luke, shocked at the disrespect from his eldest son. "I must be going deaf. What the hell did you say?"

"Dad, chill out," said Vincent, who had a more peaceful relationship with his father. It was John who always took the beatings.

"Yeah, Dad, sorry. I didn't mean anything by it," said John.

Luke gave John a stern look, one that was blinded by rage. The moment made the entire dinner awkward, and neither Michael nor Owen could tolerate it.

"Calm down, Luke. Here, have some oysters," said Owen.

"Yeah, tell us about the restaurant," added Michael. He was not scared of Luke and preferred to get under his dumber brother's skin.

"Restaurant? Nobody told me about a restaurant," said Jean Luke.

Luke had not told his father about the new venture. Jean Luke had no tolerance for his son's shenanigans. All he cared about was money and the legacy that he would leave behind. So, when Luke announced a new restaurant venture after stealing thousands of dollars from the family business, Jean Luke demanded an explanation.

"It's nothing, Dad. Michael's just talking out of his ass," said Luke to diffuse the situation.

"Nothing? Really? Charles Thies, the Miller distributor, stopped by the restaurant the other day looking for you. He said you two were partnering for a new place in Jupiter," ratted Michael.

"Luke, is this true? How are you going to pay for this? Why didn't you say anything? Aren't you going to pay me back first?" said Jean Luke.

"Dad, don't listen to this asshole. He doesn't know what he's talking about," replied Luke with the tone of a guilty son.

"I really hope you're not thinking about it, son. I won't let it happen," said Jean Luke firmly.

Joyce Thibault was on the verge of tears. Nothing tormented her more than seeing her boys fight with each other. As the years went by and the fortune grew, so did the greed. Her family had been burnt to ashes, and it took a toll on her and her husband's health.

As was always the tradition, the family gathered on the balcony for drinks and cigars after dinner. Everyone sat around a table, engaging in conversation. Luke hardly spoke, only to his mother. Owen and Michael used the time to review negotiation details with Jean Luke about a new dock being built at a restaurant.

"The city's willing to give us the permits, but the landowner doesn't want to budge. They're worried about liability," said Owen Thibault.

"We need to continue negotiating. The restaurant must have a new dock. Two-Georges is taking away our customers because they offer a dining experience on the water. This could also be the final piece that I added to the restaurant. So, I want it done said Jean Luke.

All the while, Luke's mind was trapped in its own desolation. The sound of the other Thibault men conducting business made him want to vomit. At one point, he abruptly stood up from his chair and stumbled to the sliding door to go use the bathroom.

Michael noticed his brother's condition and watched from where he sat. He watched Luke bump into a large flowering pot on the way in and struggle to light his cigar after returning. It took stubborn Luke nearly two minutes to produce a flame that could tolerate the ocean breeze.

At the same time, John and Shannon were enjoying each other's company. They never returned to talking about the heist. It appeared that John made his point, and Shannon chose to accept the circumstances. Despite knowing that he was a thief, she did not feel threatened by him in any way.

"I'm really glad I got to spend Christmas with you. For a while there, I wasn't sure what I was going to do," said Shannon.

"What about your family? What are they doing today?" asked John.

"Not much. I guess my brother and his wife will go to my mom's place, and she'll make a ham. It's pretty boring. It's always been that way," added Shannon.

"Well, there's never a dull moment when my family gets together. You just have to get used to the drunk people trying to kill each other," said John, who didn't know that his father was standing behind him, listening.

"You've got some nerve to talk shit about this family. Who the fuck do you think you are?" said an infuriated Luke.

John was caught off guard and instantly struck with concern. He turned around and saw a familiar look on his father's face, one that usually preceded a beating. But he was not a scared child anymore. All he hoped to do was diffuse the situation and prevent a violent scene.

"I didn't mean anything by it, Dad," said John. Luke was not listening to anything at that point anymore.

"What the hell are you doing with your life that's so good? You're not in college. You're high every day... you're nothing but a disappointment to me," slurred Luke.

"And you're nothing but a failure to me," replied John.

Without warning, Luke punched John's face, sending him down to a knee. Luke stood over him with his left fist clenched for a second punch. John wanted to lunge forward and wrestle his father to the ground. He had wanted to do it for a long time. But as always, he took the high road and withheld from raising his hands.

After coming to his senses, Luke put down his fist and stepped away. He looked at his stunned family before leaving disgraced. After he closed the sliding door, Shannon and Vincent walked over to help John, who was still dazed.

"Are you okay?" asked Vincent.

"Not sure, I'm a little woozy," replied John before being lifted to his feet.

John and Shannon left the condo and entered the elevator. They arrived on the first floor and walked towards the building entrance. Before stepping outside, John paused. Shannon turned around to see if he was alright.

"What's wrong," she asked.

John took a moment to collect his thoughts. He didn't want his family to poison the relationship he was developing with Shannon. She was the best thing that ever happened to him.

"I'm not a violent person, not like him. But no matter how many times he hits me, he's my father, and I'll always want to help him. Once this thing is finished, I'm going to take care of my family. And then I want us to start a life together because I love you."

"Just come back safe, and I'll be here waiting for you. From there, I'll do whatever you want, John," replied Shannon.

They walked out of the luxurious oceanside building holding hands. Shannon had witnessed the darkest side of John's life and was more attracted to him because of it. She was convinced that her strong attraction for John wasn't because she was naïve or desperate. It was simply a case of meeting the man of her destiny at that point in her life.

Chapter Sixteen

FRIDAY, DECEMBER 28th

John, Alexis, Leo, and Brian gathered at the Garcia home to discuss the heist's plan of execution. It was the early afternoon, and nobody had anywhere else to go. It was a chilly day in Florida, windy too. So, they sat in a cluttered, three-car garage that was filled with years of family memories. Leo was blasting violent music, mostly punk and rap, from his truck. Next to the truck was a mysterious white van that John and Brian had never seen.

Alexis practiced his boxing skills on the punching bag while Brian lifted some reps on the bench press. John, who was flaunting a bruised cheek and cut lip, sat on a folding chair drinking a beer. Leo finished drying a blunt with his lighter and handed it to Alexis.

"Your meeting may proceed," he said to his little brother.

Alexis and Brian each grabbed a beach chair and sat down next to the others. Alexis leaned forward to block a gust of wind with his body while lighting the blunt. He took a few puffs before passing it to John and starting the meeting.

"Okay, so here's what I got... we all need an alibi for the heist. John, you work that night, right?" asked Alexis.

"Yeah, I'm closing. We're closing at ten that night, but I can say I stayed behind doing inventory. I'll just leave everything ready a day before to make it look that way," said John.

"Why would anybody stay working on New Year's Eve? It just doesn't make sense," asked Brian.

"Because I'm depressed, my mom is suicidal, and my dad just

punched me in the face," calmly replied John.

"Cool, Leo and I will be here with the family," said Alexis before turning to Brian. "Where the fuck are you going to be?"

"I'll be in West Palm at a party. I'll make my rounds and slip out by ten," replied Brian. "That should leave me with enough time to get the boat in the water and head to the meeting spot."

"Alright, I'm going to leave all the equipment ready in the van that William provided. He's the buyer's messenger. Leo and I will ride out at ten-thirty and meet John at the Publix on the corner of Congress and Boynton. John comes with us and we head to the museum. We'll scope it out for a bit. Then Leo drops us off at eleven forty-five. That'll give us ten minutes to sprint to the back, hook our lines, get to the top, and unlock the hatch as soon as the ball drops."

"Where do I go?" asked Leo.

"Just drop off the van across the street and go wait by the bikes until we get there. We'll fly to the Intracoastal, dump the bikes, meet with Brian, and head out to open water... just don't forget to wipe down the van before you leave it," said Alexis.

It was not the most brilliant plan, but it gave the boys a puncher's chance to complete the job. Alexis had become the most confident one in the group. Maybe it was because it all sounded too simple, but the others needed reassurance that it was going to work. There were a few seconds of silence as the emotions processed in everyone's minds.

"So, what other equipment did this guy give us?" asked Brian before taking a large puff of the blunt.

They walked to the van to review the equipment. Alexis opened the sliding door and revealed the generosity of their buyer. Brian and John were instantly in disbelief at the items they saw. Only in movies did they ever see such an arsenal of crime equipment.

"We got three bikes, industrial ropes, extra grappling hooks, three bullet-proof vests, a hand-held police radio, a torch to open the hatch, night vision goggles, grappling equipment to slide down to the third floor, smoke bombs, and even a little hand grenade to open the doors in case they lock."

"Oh shit, this just got real," said John while smoking a cigarette. "So, what happens after Brian picks us up?"

"We ride out to Grand Bahama and meet the buyer at his house on Lucaya Beach. It shouldn't take us more than three hours, right Brian?" said Alexis.

"That's right, maybe less. I know how to get there pretty easily. All we gotta do is mark it on the GPS. The boat also has a backup GPS in case the first one goes out," replied Brian.

There was nothing left to say. At that point, everything was set. John and Alexis each took a grappling hook to practice their throws and get accustomed to the equipment. They practiced for three hours in the backyard, continuing to smoke and drink the entire time.

Everybody went their separate ways that evening, committed to reuniting the night of the heist. But there was a shared sense of fear among the group. They were still boys, guided by instinct and a little life experience to get the job done.

Chapter Seventeen

DECEMBER 3rd, 2001 - BOYNTON BEACH, FLORIDA

The day had arrived. After months of planning, the boys were finally going to execute their ridiculous attempt to steal the Honus Wagner baseball card. Their commitment to the plan was admirable, but they had no idea what they were getting into. The plan was a recipe for disaster. John knew it. Alexis knew it. Leo definitely knew it. But they were also young men of faith. And although they were committing a major sin by stealing, the nave catholic schoolers still put their safety and success in the hands of God.

Weiss & Fletcher Bookstore. 9:47 pm

John was waiting for the last customers to finish making their purchases. Of all the stores in the plaza, Weiss & Fletcher was the only one that stayed open during regular hours on New Year's Eve.

Shannon was also working the night shift. She and John had not spoken to each other for the entire day. They focused on their tasks while anxiously waiting for the day to end. All the while, Shannon was nervous and worried for John. But she could not conjure the confidence to try and stop him.

Throughout the day, she wandered by the music section, pretending like she was only putting books away on the shelves. She wanted to give him a chance to say something. But there was no such effort from John. He just kept his head down until everybody in the store was gone.

It was 10:20 in the evening, and John was finishing the inventory check when his alarm sounded. He put down the box he was holding and walked out of the music section towards the back exit. He passed by the bathroom, knocked on its door three times, and walked outside through the exit door. As soon as the door dosed behind him, Vincent walked out of the bathroom wearing the same clothes that John was wearing.

Further out west, the Garcia brothers were struggling to make their exit from the family party. Everybody arrived earlier than expected, all the cousins, aunts, uncles, and closest friends. As was tradition, they were all drunk, eating enormous amounts of food, and having a grand time.

Alexis and Leo were eventually pulled into the fun, but they refrained from drinking alcohol. Instead, they ate delicious Latin food and smoked a few bowls with the male cousins in the driveway. To not raise suspicion, they nursed a cup of juice to pass it off as a screwdriver.

Once all the "primos" were nice and high, Alexis and Leo slipped through the garage door and left to meet John.

John entered the Publix shopping center at 10:3 2 and saw the cargo van waiting at the far end of the parking lot. The white Escort parked next to the van and he stepped out with a bookbag in hand. He opened the van's door, stepped inside, and then closed the door. They were all dressed in burglar black.

"Let's do this," he said as he patted his friends on the shoulder.

Leo put the van's transmission into drive, and he moved out of the plaza. At first, the car ride was quiet as they all entered a focused state of mind.

"You guys want to take a few rips before we get there?" suggested a nervous John.

Alexis turned around and looked at his best friend with an indifferent look and said, "Might as well."

John took out his little pipe which was already packed with weed. He took two hits and then passed it to Alexis. After taking his two hits, he passed the pipe to Leo who lit the pipe while holding it with his teeth. He made a goofy face with each hit he took, trying to lighten the mood.

"Are you fucking ready?" Alexis asked John.

"Yeah, man, I'm fucking ready," said John. "I want to grab this fucking thing and be in the ocean within a matter of minutes. Just lead the way, Guapos. I'll do whatever the fuck you say," said John.

"Thanks, dog. We're doing everything that we rehearsed. We each packed our own backpacks at the same time. The ropes are ready. Remember, when you climb the wall, rest with your ass, and pull with your back. Don't let your arms get tired."

"I still can't believe you got me into this. You better not fuck up. Mom and Dad will kill me if you end up in jail," added Leo.

The closer they got to the Delray/Boca border, the more nervous they all became. After passing Linton Boulevard, they knew the museum was seconds away on the left.

"There it is. It's fucking go time," said John.

Leo drove to the drop-off point for the bikes along the hedges behind the museum's property perimeter. John stepped out of the van, took out the bikes, and rested them against the hedges. Then Alexis grabbed the supply bags from the back of the van and closed the door. He approached the driver-side window and said to his brother, "Alright, man, drop off the van across the street, and I'll see you here in ten minutes."

As Leo drove away, Alexis' phone buzzed. It was a text message from Brian that read: *Pulling in, tying up.*

"Okay, man, you ready?" Alexis said to John.

"Yeah, bro. Lead the way," replied John as fireworks burst in the distance. Then Alexis started the countdown.

"Three, two, one... go!" said Alexis.

They put on their masks and sprinted to the museum's back wall. In almost synchronous fashion, John and Alexis dropped their bags and grabbed their ropes and grappling hooks.

"I can't fucking believe this," was all John could say as he reviewed his rope setup one last time.

"Believe it. That card is ours," replied Alexis.

As the clock neared midnight, the fireworks activity from nearby neighborhoods increased. Alexis gripped the end of the rope that met the grappling hook and started to spin the contraption counterclockwise to gain momentum for the throw. At the same time, he held the rope's slack in his left hand. He needed a strong release to clear all three levels of the building. John closely watched Alexis' form and started to do the same.

After a few seconds, Alexis threw his grappling hook in the air and attempted to direct its trajectory. It was a tense moment for both Alexis and John to see the hook glide against gravity. But to their surprise, the throw was perfectly executed on the first attempt. The grappling hook cleared the roof and locked on the building's ledge after Alexis pulled it.

"Whoa, nice throw," said John, who was still swinging his rope to maintain momentum.

He followed Alexis's lead and tossed the hook in the air with all his strength. He followed the hook with his eyes until it landed on the roof. Then he pulled the rope to secure the hook. After giving a few extra tugs, he confirmed to Alexis that he was ready to climb the building.

"It's hooked. Let's climb," he said.

They walked up to the wall of the building, gripped the rope firmly, and wrapped it around their forearms.

"It's 11:50. We gotta get up there quick. Remember, dude, use the notches. Lean on your ass and let your back do all the work," said Alexis.

"Got it, race you to the top," said John before beginning his ascent.

The two friends, being young and agile, had no problem scaling the wall of the building. It was surprisingly easy for them to do so. When Alexis got to the top, he grabbed the ledge with his right hand and pulled himself onto the roof. Then he turned around and helped his friend do the same.

They left the ropes and grappling hooks on the wall and ran to the hatch door. Alexis searched for a lock around its edges but struggled to find it. Meanwhile, John took a second to absorb the view from the top of the building. The sky over Palm Beach County radiated with bursts of fireworks. Nonstop, there were blasting, popping, and crackling sounds. There were even a few pops that sounded like gunfire.

"There's no lock. I brought the torch, but we're not even going to need it," he told John while smiling.

"He probably never thought anyone would be crazy enough to break in through the roof," replied John.

Alexis gripped the handle and lifted the door with hardly any effort. He could see all the way to the first floor and confirmed the drop point underneath.

"Alright, take out your second rope. We'll drop straight onto the third floor and probably set off the alarm along the way. That's why we gotta be quick," said Alexis.

John took out the second rope, a harness, his number eight ring, and a carabiner clip. Although they had rehearsed the process multiple times, he still opted to follow Alexis' steps.

"Okay, grab your eight-ring. Pass the rope through the big loop and around the smaller loop. Now, clip the harness and the carabiner together. Make sure to clip the carabiner through the rope, so your line doesn't knot," said Alexis. John did as was instructed. He secured both ends of the rope, setting it up to rappel down to the third floor.

They threw one end of the rope down the hatch and tied the other end to a safety bar using a Prusik knot. After giving a few hard tugs, they confirmed that the rope was securely tied.

"Ready?" asked Alexis.

"Ready," confirmed John.

"I'll hang first, and then you follow my lead. It's better if the alarms go off when we're both going down," said Alexis.

With nothing but blind confidence in his mind, Alexis leaned above the hatch opening and let himself hang with the harness. He looked at his watch to check the time as John joined him. At that point, both friends were hanging from the roof of the museum, with only fifty feet of air separating them from the baseball card. John took a couple of deep breaths while Alexis started the countdown.

"Five, four, three, two... one," said Alexis. "Happy fucking new year, buddy!"

The fireworks show throughout the county intensified at the stroke of midnight. With his left hand, he released the bottom side of the rope, allowing it to slip through the eight-ring, which let him descend. After only twenty feet, the sensors set off the alarm. John took notice, did the sign of the cross, and rappelled down with Alexis.

They landed on the third floor and unlatched their harnesses. Alexis was the first to get free and immediately sprinted toward the baseball card display. The piercing alarm sound did little to jolt his focus.

Alexis placed his hands on the side of the display and lifted the protective glass cover. He was surprised to see how easy it was. The boy took a few seconds to grasp what was happening. They could not believe the card was theirs for the taking.

"So, now I just grab it, and we go," said Alexis while handing John the glass case. But their escape would not be so easy, for a cynical business owner lurked in the shadows.

"Don't you fucking move! I've got both of you locked. You try anything, and you're dead," said Herb Bowman.

He stepped out of the shadows holding a leashed mastiff in his right hand and a nine-millimeter pistol in the other hand. Luckily, Alexis and John were wearing masks, so Herb could not immediately identify them.

Over by the hedges, Leo could see through the windows. But he could only see the south side of the first floor and had no view of the second or third floor. While waiting nervously for them to run through the front door, he listened to a hand-held police radio. But nothing had been reported by dispatch.

"Fuck, hurry up, guys," he said to himself.

The mastiff was enormous and looked mean. The beast stood on all fours, with its back arched, ready to attack the moment Herb commanded. Alexis knew he needed to act quickly. But he also didn't want to get John killed in the process.

"Now, this is what's going to happen," said Herb with a somewhat sadistic look on his face. "You boys are going to take off your masks and lie face down on the ground until the cops arrive. Otherwise, old Zeus here will tear you to pieces."

"No problem, we'll do what you say," said Alexis before looking at John and nodding his head.

"I know exactly who you two are," said Herb Bowman with his gun pointed. "Where are the rest of your buddies?"

"There's nobody else;' said John to take the attention off Alexis.

"Hurry up, masks off, now!" said Herb.

John kept his hands in the air to distract Herb. Alexis acted like he was about to take off his mask with his right hand. Just as his mouth unveiled, John started ranting to Herb.

"Hey, Herb! Fuck you! You fat fucking piece of shit!"

John got Herb Bowman's full attention after that. It allowed Alexis to make his move. After Herb pointed his gun at John, Alexis pulled the pin from a smoke bomb. Herb took notice of the smoke and pointed the gun at Alexis. John took advantage of the distraction, grabbed a displayed baseball, and beamed it at Herb's face. He released Zeus and fired a shot into the air. The smoke became thick, giving John and Alexis a cover to escape.

Zeus bit John's leg and dropped him to the ground. But John's momentum allowed him to pull away and sprint towards the stairs. Alexis grabbed him, and they both disappeared into the smoke.

When Herb came to his senses, he put his hands on his face and discovered blood across his nose. The cloud of smoke made it hard for him to see anything else in the vicinity. But he could hear John and Alexis running down the stairs.

Once Herb saw Alexis running towards the door, he emptied the clip of his gun, firing multiple shots at the boys. Luckily for Alexis, Herb was a terrible shot. John and Alexis juiced and swiveled around the displays with their heads down as bullets flew.

Pumped full of adrenaline, Alexis charged the building's door with all his momentum but was unable to get it open. He slammed on the door and bounced off with the same amount of force. That was when Zeus sought his opportunity.

The mastiff grabbed Alexis's arm with his powerful jaw and jolted it from side to side. Alexis screamed bloody murder while trying to get loose. Luckily for him, John saw an opening and kicked Zeus's belly with all his strength. The dog howled in pain and immediately released Alexis's arm before disappearing to the back. With no other choice, both friends jumped behind the front register to evade getting shot.

"Ha, I got you little shits trapped!" yelled Herb before making his way downstairs. Alexis took out his phone to send Leo a text message. Leo's interference was their only chance to escape.

"You thought you could pull a fast one on Herb Bowman!" said Herb while casually walking down the stairs. "I didn't get this far in life by being a sucker. Thibault, I know it's you! Along with your Mexican friend!"

John and Alexis looked at each other, scared that they were finally going to get caught. Just then, they could hear police sirens in the distance. At that moment, it seemed as though the entire heist would be nothing but a failure.

Herb arrived at the first floor and walked towards the entrance booth. To keep the boys scared, he shot twice into the air.

"Your family's going to owe me big, Thibault. Maybe I'll take over one of those snazzy restaurants," said Herb.

Suddenly, the van screeched onto the parking lot and drove straight towards the entrance door. It smashed through with full force, blasting items and debris into the air. Herb Bowman was caught in the path of the van and could not move out of the way in time. It was not a direct hit, but the van's right fender sent him crashing to the ground.

"Where y'all at!?" yelled Leo from the van.

They lifted their heads from behind the register and acknowledged the disaster area. John saw Herb underneath a clutter of items and debris. He wasn't moving at all.

"Did you get the card!?" yelled Leo after stepping out of the van.

"Yeah," replied Alexis, who was in shock.

"Well, let's fucking go!" suggested Leo as the police sirens got louder.

With Herb Bowman unconscious and Zeus scared behind some corner, John, Alexis, and Leo ran out of that museum. They sprinted to the hedges and passed through the opening where the bikes were parked. They each mounted a bike and rode down the street to the Intracoastal Waterway as fast as possible.

"Dude, what made you go get the van?" asked John while pedaling vigorously.

"Heard the gunshots... knew I had to blast those doors... open," huffed and puffed Leo.

They were halfway down the street when the police arrived at the museum. John turned around and could see the massive flash of red and blue lights. He scoped the neighborhood after that to see if any residents were outside seeing the lights or celebrating. But they were lucky. Nobody was outside.

They got to the end of the street, where Brian was waiting in the boat. John and Alexis dropped their bikes in the water. Mighty Leo threw his bike as far as he could while hollering loudly, "Aaarrrgh!"

"What's up, man? Good to see you," said Alexis. "You too, bro," said Brian.

Once everyone was in the boat, Alexis and Leo untied the ropes from the cleats and pushed off the wall. At the same time, a helicopter could be seen arriving at the crime scene. Brian wasted no time leaving the area. He steered the boat and accelerated north towards the Boynton inlet. Once they were heading in the right direction, John, Alexis, and Leo took off the burglar clothes and threw them in the water.

They quickly changed into casual clothing and took a seat to finally relax. The Garcia brothers sat on the rear seats while John joined Brian in the center console. All the while, fireworks continued to blast in the air all along the Intracoastal.

"Did you get it?" Brian asked John, who was exhausted beyond imagination.

"I think so," replied John. He turned around to confirm with Alexis. "Hey, Guapos, you do have the card, right?"

Alexis snapped out of his train of thought. He was also exhausted and needed a second to absorb everything that had just happened.

"Alexis, do you have the card!" repeated John, speaking over the sound of the engine.

"Yeah, man. I got it right here," replied Alexis while tapping his leg pocket.

"Let's see it," said Brian.

"Alright, but nobody can touch it. I don't want any of you assholes dropping it into the water or anything... hand me a light," said Alexis. Brian handed him a small flashlight from the center console's storage space.

He took the card out of his zipper pocket and first showed it to Leo, who was sitting next to him. Alexis held the protective box tightly with both hands to prevent it from slipping or falling into the water.

"That's it? All this for that?" complained Leo. "I think I saw one of those in a Cracker Jack box once."

Alexis rolled his eyes and said, "That was just a replica that's worth nothing. We got more than two million dollars right here."

John was the next to take a look. He got up from the center-console seat and stepped to the stern. He acknowledged the importance of the moment, one full of awe and inspiration. He also could not believe what they had accomplished, not for a second. But there it was, proof of mankind's capabilities.

"When did you grab it?" asked John.

"When that fucking dog was gnawing on your leg replied Alexis. "I couldn't see because of the smoke, so I just reached for it."

John grabbed the wheel while Brian took his opportunity to see the card. He had no interest in baseball, so he could not appreciate the degree of its rarity. He only wanted to witness the underlying cause of all their efforts.

"That fucking thing is worth two million?" asked Brian.

"That's right, man. This little fucking card with an ugly white dude on it is worth two million dollars," replied Alexis. "And as long as everything goes well, I think we're each adding an additional ten grand to your cut."

"What!?" Leo quickly expressed. "I'm not giving any money to this honky."

"Why's it got to be a race thing?" replied Brian jokingly. "We couldn't have done it without you. It's only fair," said Alexis.

Brian returned to the steering wheel as the others sat quietly to wander in thought. The idle cruise to the Boynton inlet gave me plenty of time to think of new possibilities.

John thought about buying a massive supply of weed, selling it, and using the profits to marry Shannon. Brian thought about starting a landscaping business. Just him, his tractor, and the open field. Leo thought about buying himself a new four-by-four truck. And Alexis thought about going on a sabbatical after college.

The boat eventually reached the outskirts of the Boynton inlet. Brian idled slowly around the markers to avoid calling attention to ocean patrol. Luckily, the inlet park had plenty of lights to help him steer clearly. His only concern was the inlet channel where there weren't any lights. There, they would encounter mighty swells and thrashing waves from the ocean. The jetty was narrow and required precision navigation to avoid crashing into the rocks.

"Alright, everyone, we're coming up to the channel. Hold on to something. This shit's going to be rough," said Brian.

"Why the fuck did you choose Boynton? You should have gone to the Boca inlet," said Leo.

"Nope, it's closed, under construction," said a focused Brian. "Just sit back and hold the fuck on, Augustus!" It was an old nickname given to Leo based on the Willy Wonka character.

The twenty-two-foot Proline was not the best boat to take through a dangerous channel like the Boynton inlet, not at night. It was a new boat with two 250 horsepower, 4-stroke Tohatsu engines. But Brian expected the possibility of water entering the boat. He would have to navigate quickly through the narrow jetty to get them out safely.

As they entered the channel, some fishermen and other onlookers were staring at the boat in shock. A slack-jawed redneck even yelled, "Turn around... you crazy asshole! Turn around!"

But the boat moved forward, under the A1A overpass, and into the darkness. The boat rocked with every wave that crashed against the hull. So, Brian accelerated to fight the current. It was during one of those jumps that the boat shot higher into the air than anticipated, almost tossing John into the water. He held on to a bar to avoid falling overboard.

As expected, the boat started to take in water as the waves rose above the gunwale. All John, Alexis, and Leo could do was hold on to dear life and pray for survival.

The boat arrived at the jetty, where Brian needed to make a sharp turn. The only light to guide him came from the moon and stars, so he could barely see where the violent waters crashed against the massive rocks.

"Hold the fuck on!" yelled Brian as he turned the wheel to make the sharp turn. He moved the throttle forward, and the boat accelerated with all its power. Within seconds, it jumped two large waves and cleared through the jetty without sustaining damage. They arrived at the ocean, officially marking the impossible heist as a successful reality.

Chapter Eighteen

The ocean conditions were favorable, considering it was winter. Brian sped the boat through the mild swells to get them to Freeport as fast as possible. There was a cool chill in the air that was exaggerated by the sea mist flying everywhere.

"Be careful, don't let it get wet," Leo told Alexis while passing him the blunt.

Alexis covered the blunt with his hands while simultaneously taking a few hits. Then he stood up to pass it to John and Brian. They were being responsible, keeping an eye out for ocean debris.

"Here, bro, take it," said Alexis as he handed the blunt to John.

"Hey, let me sit back there for a second. I want to rest my back," said John after taking a hit.

John and Alexis switched places, putting Alexis in the center console with Brian. It was the first time in a long time that there was no unspoken tension between the two. It felt like the way things were when they had a friendship based on trust and loyalty.

"If anyone could pull something like this off, it was always you. Even when we were little and decided to break into those old people's houses, you went for it, and we got all that jewelry. Now we're international thieves," said Brian.

"Yeah, but like always, you played a vital role. We wouldn't have gotten into that house if you didn't break the lock with that screwdriver," reminded Alexis.

"Damn, man! It's really good to chill like this again... I'm sorry for betraying you. I don't know what the fuck I was thinking," said

Brian.

"... Yeah, I didn't expect that. I don't think we can ever be friends again, not like before. But I do accept your apology," said Alexis.

"Was it that bad... what I did?" asked Brian, who was hurt by the response. "I let you try to fuck Jen that one night."

"Yeah, and if I knew what was happening, I would've joined you. As long as you didn't touch me," replied Alexis.

He pointed to John and said, "You see that motherfucker right there, that's a fucking friend. He's loyal. I can trust him. When I needed a friend, he was there. You forgot all about that, Brian. And I don't think people change. So, I can never trust you again."

"I guess that's just the way it is," replied Brian.

After two hours of riding the waters, it seemed they were on easy street. The boat was cruising in record time to Grand Bahama. There wasn't much conversation on that boat because everyone was exhausted. There was a lot to process for those young minds. They had just committed the crime of the century and were about to become rich overnight. But the job wasn't finished, and they had no idea who the buyer was or where they were going.

At some point, John noticed storm clouds in the distance. As Brian continued to accelerate, it became that there was no escaping the rain.

"You're going to drive through the storm?" he asked Brian.

"We don't have a choice. So, hold on," said Brian before accelerating faster.

At first, they were hit by a few sprinkles of rain. But the waters became rough. Everyone held on tight as the boat jumped choppy waves. And then the water started to pour, pelleting Alexis and Leo with stinging raindrops. But Brian kept his focus on driving them out of the storm.

His confidence helped to keep the others calm, and so did the boat's performance. It was seemingly gliding through the waves, making the experience more tolerable for everyone. And after almost ten minutes, they could see the other side of the storm. The rain eventually stopped falling, and the waters calmed. Brian had successfully driven them through a mild storm.

"Hey! I gotta take a fucking piss!" yelled Leo to Brian.

"Me too," said John.

"Well, let's all take a piss then," said Brian. He lowered the throttle and stopped the boat somewhere in the middle of the Atlantic Ocean. Everybody chose a corner to have a private moment. Brian and Alexis faced the east, while Leo and John faced the west.

There was no sight of land and no lights in either direction. There was just the ocean, the night sky, the moon, and the stars. A more peaceful setting was nearly impossible to imagine. That was until the wind blew Alexis's piss on Leo.

"Hey, hey, hey! What the fuck!?" said Leo aloud while trying not to pee on himself.

When everyone was relieved, they returned to their seats to finish the rest of the trip. The GPS indicated that they were less than one hour away from the island. At least, that's what they thought until Brian flipped the ignition button, and the engine didn't start. It was somewhat terrifying to everyone to see that happen. Brian tried to flip on the switch a second time, and again, the engine didn't start. Then he tried a third time, only to get the same result.

"What's up, man?" Alexis asked Brian.

"The fucking engine doesn't start," he replied.

That was the most frightening thing anyone could hear in open waters, especially when there was a strong current.

"Both of them?" asked Alexis.

"Yep, both," confirmed Brian.

"What the fuck do you mean?" asked John.

"I don't know... I don't know," said Brian in a nervous tone as he examined the dashboard. "This shit shouldn't be happening."

Leo assisted Brian with the flashlight as he checked the battery and its connections. John and Alexis waited anxiously while staring out into the ocean. All the while, the boat rocked to the left and to the right, reminding everyone how utterly helpless they were out there.

"So, what if he can't fix it?" Alexis asked Leo. "Should we swim?"

"It'll be a good workout," jokingly replied Leo.

"You wouldn't go anywhere with that current," said John.

"I don't know. Leo's on a couple of different steroid cycles right now. I think he could swim for hours," added Alexis as Leo flexed his twenty-inch arms.

Time lingered as Brian searched for a solution to the engine problem. Alexis stared at the water and focused on the crystal glare from the moonlight. The refraction was blinding at times but still a majestic sight to see. Out in the distance, about one hundred feet away, he noticed a school of fish migrating eastward. The moonlight gave a clear showing of the water ripples the fish created.

Leo made another observation. While waiting nervously for Brian to deliver good news, he noticed a dark shadow briefly skim out of the water. The figure was real enough to keep his attention. It then disappeared under the water, leaving Leo with an ardent desire to see it again. When the figure re-emerged, it was a lot closer to the boat. Still, Leo could not confirm what it was, but it looked a lot like a shark fin.

"Fuck that... I'll take my chances in the boat," said Leo to Alexis.

Some minutes later, Brian was able to identify and fix the problem. He closed the center console's compartment door where the ignition system was located. Leo turned off the flashlight, and Brian returned to the steering wheel.

"Let's hope this works," he said before turning the key.

The engines started, and John gave a sigh of relief. Leo and Alexis lifted their heads like startled dogs. Brian listened keenly to the motor before determining that everything was running smoothly.

"Alright, we're back in the game! Let's get the fuck out of here," said Brian. He moved the throttle forward and continued towards Freeport.

After thirty minutes of riding, they could start to see lights emerging on the horizon. They were still about twenty miles out, but the twinkling lights of the port were a welcoming relief to see.

"Is that it?" asked John.

"I'm pretty sure. But my GPS says we have to go in through the south side of the island," replied Brian. That required them to veer further south to enter through the bay.

The number of lights became more abundant the further they progressed. Although Brian did not head directly toward them, it was comforting for everyone to know that they were that close to land.

Brian followed the GPS to the south side of the island. They passed Lucaya and Taino Beach before spotting the buoy lights for the Fortune Beach inlet. Again, they would have to navigate a rough current to pass the jetty, but it was wider than and not as dangerous as the Boynton inlet. Brian maintained a low wake until the rip current started to rock the boat. At that point, he accelerated and crossed the danger zone within a few seconds.

They entered Millionaire's Row, where Grand Bahama's richest residents lived. The water in the channel was calm, and the house lights marked where to go. Everyone on that boat was nervous as they had no idea who the buyer was. Still, Alexis grabbed his phone and called William, who was on standby at the buyer's house.

"Alex! You here, mate?" said William in his thick English accent. He was standing poolside at the buyer's property, holding a whiskey in his left hand.

"William! Hey, we're in Millionaire's Row," replied Alexis.

"I can't believe you boys fucking did it. Look in the sky. I'm shooting a flare from the property. Just come up to the dock. I'll be here waiting," said William.

William grabbed a flare gun from his back pocket, pointed it in the air, and fired a shot. The flare zoomed directly above the house, and Alexis spotted it within seconds.

"That's the flare. It should be around the next corner," said Alexis to Brian.

As the boat navigated to the final location, Leo was getting ready for potential sabotage. He was the muscle of the group and intended to act upon that role if needed. He put brass knuckles and a knife in one pocket and the nine-millimeter pistol in the other pocket. Then he handed his brother the revolver.

"Here, take this. We gotta keep our eyes open," said Leo. "Thanks, bro, no doubt," replied Alexis.

He put the gun in the waistband of his jeans and held the baseball card in his left pocket. All the while, John observed the Garcia brothers' preparation. He questioned if the guns were necessary. He could not bear the thought of seeing somebody die, especially one of his friends. Nonetheless, he felt safe to have the Garcia brothers by his side.

Brian followed the flare and turned into a canal. He noticed a home about fifty yards away with two red lights flashing on the roof. He looked at the GPS and confirmed the property as their destination. With little idea as to what or who waited for them, the four youngsters from Boynton Beach arrived at the lavish home ready to finalize the deal.

William was standing on the deck with a drink in one hand and a cigarette in the other. He put the cigarette in his mouth and threw a rope to Leo to tie the bow. That was the signal for Brian to turn off the engine. John grabbed the dock along the stern, jumped out, and tied the rope to a cleat.

"Welcome, welcome. You boys have done well. I wasn't sure if you'd make it, but here you are," said William.

It was almost four in the morning. Everyone stepped off the boat, tired but relieved to be on steady land. Despite that, Alexis couldn't allow himself to lose focus. He had a plan of getting in and out as quickly as possible.

"You got the card?" asked William.

"We got it. But I have to see the money first," replied Alexis.

"Hey, buddy, we're all in good company here," replied William.

"I know, William. But I just want to put this in your boss's hands, grab our pay, and go," said Alexis with his bros standing tall behind him.

"Alright, no problem. I get it. You did your part, so follow me," said William, who sensed the seriousness of Alexis's tone.

Chapter Nineteen

It was a dream home. Like all the other mansions, the property had a large backyard that extended all the way to the ocean canal. But unlike the other mansions, the buyer's home had thick vegetation of tall trees in a meshed arrangement.

"Welcome to the Grand Bahama Bird Sanctuary. Mrs. Loretta is a world-renowned bird researcher. She bought this place twenty years ago and built it into a national 'park. Hundreds of species gather here during the winter months, leaving the boss plenty occupied."

"Mrs. Loretta?" said John.

"That's right... Oh, did I forget to tell you that my boss is a woman?" replied William.

"Really? A chick? I thought you mentioned that your boss was a man. What the hell does a woman want with a baseball card?" asked Alexis.

"Well, Alex, my boy, that's mighty sexist of you to say. But I guess you're about to find out," said William.

William guided them down a dark path through the dense landscape. There were no lights in the sanctuary. It was only meant to be experienced during the day. Their feet stepped over dirt, rocks, woodchips, and other natural foliage. As they got closer to the house, some lights started to emerge above the shadows.

"Uh, where the fuck are you taking us?" asked Leo.

"Just a few more steps, boys. We're good," replied William.

They passed through the bird sanctuary and arrived at the mansion's backyard patio. It was more bizarre than the private eco-forest. There was an enclosure with 'multiple animal kennels. The area of the enclosure was as big as a small garage, with various stairwells and compartments built within.

The rest of the home and patio had a modest look, a concrete base with potted plants everywhere. The house was colored white with a Spanish tile roof. It was far different than the lavish gangster home Alexis imagined.

"What's with the fucking cages?" asked John.

"That's for the Mrs.'s cats. She has about thirty rescues on the property," said William as they arrived at the front door. "Wait here."

William walked inside the house through a sliding glass door. John, Alexis, Leo, and Brian waited with curiosity. They eyeballed the property and the cats that emerged into the light. There were all sorts of moans and 'meows coming from the enclosure, which startled the boys. None of them were cat lovers.

"Fuck these things. How come we haven't left yet?" said Brian.

"Exactly," said Alexis.

They waited for nearly ten minutes until the sliding door finally opened, and William re-emerged.

"Hey, boys! Come on in," he said.

"Hey!" yelled Alexis. "What the fuck is this? I wanted to be fueled and gone by now."

"My guys have already fueled your tank. We'd like to conduct business inside if you all don't mind," said William.

Everyone turned to Leo to see what he suggested. He was the toughest of the group and had the biggest gun. He did not want to ruin the business opportunity, especially because they'd come so far. He shook his head in disappointment at the way things were going, shrugged his shoulders, and motioned the others to enter the house.

"It's like you don't trust your old friend, William. I wouldn't have given you that pistol in big man's pocket if we were planning to kill you," said a lighthearted 'William as the others entered the house.

They walked into the living room, which had two illuminated lamps. It was a large room that was cluttered with furniture, boxes, books, and a few cats. The tables were covered with nature magazines, mail, cat bowls, and other random junk.

John was growing nervous. They were all at the mercy of the buyer, and he could only pray that it was not a setup. Leo stood firm next to his brother, watching William as he strolled back and forth, biting his nails.

"Say, man? What's going on here? Where's your boss?" asked an impatient Leo.

William was startled by Leo's brashness. But he looked at him and said, "Just a minute, mate. I promise. You'll be on your way."

Just then, an elderly woman walked into the room. Everyone assumed it was the buyer, Mrs. Loretta because she was dressed like a birder. She wore light clothing, a multi-pocketed khaki vest, and comfortable walking shoes. She was looking for something, as though getting ready to leave the house for the day. William let her browse for a minute before grabbing her attention.

"Mrs. Julia, the boys are here with the delivery."

The septuagenarian seemed confused and still groggy from the early hours. But she heard William and replied by saying, "My dear, you know I can't go on the trail without my binoculars. I know I set them here last night, somewhere."

"I think I saw them in the kitchen," replied William.

"Well, then, I am definitely losing my mind because I was just in there," said Julia Loretta, the esteemed bird watcher.

She looked at the young men with bewildered looks on their faces and said, "I had my doubts about you boys. Based on William's description, you had no idea what you were doing."

Underneath that quiet setting in the middle of the ocean, Alexis dropped his sense of urgency and opted to properly address the old woman.

"That's the problem with old people. They think young people can't do anything. Guys like us were born for this, 'ma'am. So, although our plan seemed novice, we took all the right steps to get it done and deliver the product as promised... plus, it would have been impossible without your help... which we already knew."

Mrs. Julia Loretta was left dumbfounded by Alexis's intelligent response. She was impressed and willing to admit that she was wrong.

"I stand corrected... do you have the card?" she asked.

"Yes, do you have the money?" asked Alexis.

All eyes were on Mrs. Loretta to see how she'd respond. With no hesitation, she looked at the boys and then looked at William, who waited for her instructions.

"William, will you show these young men their money," said Julia.

'William put a sucker in his mouth and did as he was instructed. He pulled out two briefcases from behind the couch, placed them on the table, and opened them.

"There it is, one-point-five million... seven hundred and fifty thousand dollars in each case," said Julia.

Alexis reached into his pocket and pulled out the baseball card. He held it in his hands for a second, staring at its details one last time. Then he put the card on the table and looked at Mrs. Julia Loretta. He noticed an immediate effect on her state of being. She could not take her eyes off the card.

"One T206 Honus Wagner baseball card," said Alexis.

Mrs. Julia Loretta kept her eyes locked on the card as she approached the table. She was speechless. William had never seen her in such a state, but he knew the reason for it. Mrs. Loretta's connection to the world's most expensive baseball card was personal. She could not believe that it was once again in her possession.

"Why are you so interested in this card?" asked John.

Mrs. Loretta picked up the card and observed it with a keen eye. It was like she was looking for something familiar. Her eyes remained in a trance until she spotted the detail and smiled.

"Did you boys know that destiny brought us all together?" she said in a calm voice.

"Why do you say that?" asked John.

"Because Mr. Herb Bowman, the man you stole this from, stole the card from my late husband. And now... you've returned it," revealed Mrs. Loretta.

"That's not what the books say. I thought he won it at an auction," said Alexis.

"My Arthur and Mr. Bowman were avid collectors of sports memorabilia. Arthur only held a few collectibles, but they were some of the most coveted items in the world. Herb, on the other hand, got his hands on every collectible that he could. And after years of knowing each other, they became business partners in real estate," said Julia.

As intriguing as the story was, John and Alexis were desperate to leave. They had annoyed looks on their faces but still maintained their southern manners. All they wanted to do was ensure possession of the cash and be on their way back to Florida.

"One day, he presented Arthur with a proposition to obtain forty percent ownership of the business. Arthur saw it as an opportunity to expand with a known associate. So, against my wishes, he signed that stupid contract. At first, he was happy with the new influx of business that Herb delivered. He was hoping to retire in five years and sell his remaining shares to Herb. But we soon found out the consequences of doing business with that serpent."

"Arthur presented Herb with a proposal to buy two blocks of low-income houses in Lake Worth. Herb supported the plan and introduced Arthur to a contractor he knew to handle the project. But the man wasn't licensed, and Herb knew it. Once the city inspectors discovered what was happening, they halted the entire project and eventually ceased the properties. Since Arthur was the primary stakeholder of the corporation, he was held responsible and had to pay the state millions of dollars in fines," said Julia.

"Herb Bowman sued Arthur after that, claiming negligence for not personally verifying the contractor's license. After working with a mediator, they decided to sell off the remaining assets of the company to pay off the city and Herb. But when Arthur was still short on what he owed, he decided to throw in his T206 card. Herb used his connections in the sports memorabilia world to make it look as though he won the card in an auction. And the rest was history. My husband died a broken man."

"Sorry to say it, but your husband was a sucker. Sounds like Herb was playing him for that card the entire time," said Brian in his youthful language.

"Yeah, and I don't know what any of this has to do with destiny. But I guess it worked out for everyone," said Alexis.

"It surely did," said Julia.

"But how did you know that we were stealing this card?" asked Alexis.

"Like I said, it was destiny. Through my own efforts, I've been able to monetize my earnings from my profession in various ways. And I've always known where the card was being held and always kept an ear out for anyone crazy enough to take it. One day, William, who is also my nephew and manager, approached me with your idea. He said there were some boys from Boynton Beach who wanted to steal a baseball card worth two-million dollars. Part of me took a chance when I told him to fund your efforts. But in my heart, I knew this was probably the only opportunity to get Arthur's card back. It's rare to find anyone crazy enough to attempt what you did," said Julia.

"If you have the money, why didn't you just buy it back from him?" asked John.

"Because I tried once before, and he told me it had become a family heirloom. He intended to pass it on to his children. You boys and your imagination created the opportunity I needed to destroy Mr. Bowman and regain 'my Arthur's baseball card," said Julia.

The boys returned to the boat when the sun was just starting to rise. But the sunlight was not going to last long as storm clouds were assembling around the island. Thanks to Julia's workers, everything was ready for the journey home. They had food, gas, and water.

Alexis held onto the briefcases with intensity and dedication. He tied one end of a rope around his wrist, and the other end around the briefcase handles. He was the first to get into the boat, followed by Leo, John, and Brian.

The boys quietly took their seats, John next to Brian and the Garcia brothers near the engines. William untied the ropes and waved goodbye as Brian steered towards the ocean. Although it was nice to have the money, they all knew the mission was not finished until they got back to Florida. Nobody wanted to celebrate prematurely.

Chapter Twenty

The storm was merciless. Within twenty minutes of leaving the Fortune Beach inlet, the boat was navigating through frightening conditions. Simultaneously, thick droplets of rain fell rapidly from the clouds, drenching everything and everyone in the boat. Brian had to rely on all his years of experience to control the vessel's balance.

There was a shared sense of fear among the boys. The massive swells rocked the boat to a tipping point. They were constantly taking in water, causing Alexis to hold the briefcases on his lap.

"Hey, man! Maybe we should head back to Freeport and wait for this shit to die down!" said John to Brian.

"This will pass. Besides, we gotta be back as quickly as possible! My dad doesn't know I took the boat, and I don't want the dock master calling him with the news that it's missing," replied Brian.

"Are you fucking sure the boat can handle this!?" added Alexis, who overheard Brian's statement.

"We'll be fine!" yelled young Brian.

The conditions worsened the further they got from the island. Leo became highly concerned over the safety of Alexis. As the older brother, he felt consumed by his protective instinct and felt incapable of controlling anything about their situation.

"Sit tight, little dude! We'll be home soon," yelled Leo through the gust and rain.

Everyone held on to whatever was available as Brian

accelerated and decelerated to fight through the waves. His biggest fear was that the boat would capsize and throw everyone into the water.

John struggled to maintain balance during Brian's navigation. He almost fell overboard when a powerful wave smashed the boat. His foot hit the edge of a rod holder, leaving a deep gash on his ankle.

"Ah! Fuck!" he yelled.

"Bro, let's go back! This shit's too strong!" yelled Alexis to Brian as the conditions got worse.

"We gotta drive through it! We gotta get back!" said Brian as the bow dipped under a wave.

"Don't fucking kill us!" yelled John.

Another wave popped Leo out of his chair and almost into the water. After regaining his balance, he stood up and opened the center console's compartment door. He reached inside, grabbed the lifejackets, and handed them to Brian and John. Then he returned to his seat and handed one to Alexis.

"Put this shit on… right now!" said Leo.

Alexis did as he was told, but there was a problem. He could not fit the suitcases through the lifejacket's armhole. So, he settled with only putting his left arm through the hole and connecting the tightening belts around his torso.

"Better than nothing," he said after observing how ridiculous he looked.

The rain poured for the next thirty minutes until it suddenly stopped. From one second to the next, they were no longer being pelleted with raindrops. But the ocean was still furious. Brian did his best to navigate the swells and still maintained hope that the worst would soon pass.

"I'm just going to get us through this rough point, and then we should be fine. But, hold on," said Brian as he accelerated.

His confidence was nothing more than blind pride. The swells were tossing the boat around like a small toy. They were completely helpless in the middle of that ocean, at God's mercy. Alexis and Leo both made the sign of the cross and started to pray.

"I just want to say... that you're a stupid motherfucker... and... we're gonna die because of you!" yelled Leo to Brian.

Leo feared the worst. He was convinced that Brian was navigating them toward a meaningless death.

"If this shit flips... you jump!" Leo yelled to his brother.

"You got that, John!?" Alexis projected the advice to his friend. John turned around to confirm his understanding with a stern look and a nod.

John thought of Shannon as death loomed. He stared as Far East as he could, knowing that his new life with her was only a few hours away. He foresaw a peaceful and beautiful future with her. He felt the warmth that she brought to his life and refused to accept they would die in that storm.

And then, an enormous swell formed to the right, about fifty feet from the boat. Brian could not keep his eye off it. It was approaching at an angle which he knew the boat would not withstand. So, in the face of uncertainty, he decided to accelerate through the wave before it crashed over the boat.

"Hold on, guys! We have to go for it!" yelled Brian. But his timing was all wrong. The boat's bow could not reach the wave's apex before it broke and flipped backward, sending everyone flying into the water. The boat had completely capsized, and the boys were scattered somewhere in the treacherous waters.

The first person to emerge out of the water was Leo. He could not see anything or anyone, causing him to panic for fear that something bad had happened to his little brother.

"Alex! Alex!" Leo yelled frantically while treading water.

He turned around and saw the boat's hull sticking out of the water, but nobody else was visible. After the longest seconds of his life, he heard something splashing toward the boat. It was John. He was unharmed and trying to reach the vessel for safety.

On the other side of the boat, Brian was doing the same. He lifted himself out of the water and onto the hull, still wearing his life jacket. The only person unaccounted for was Alexis.

"Alex!" yelled Leo for a third time, fearing his brother was dead.

There was no immediate response. The longer he waited for one, the further he drifted from the boat. Alexis was still underwater. He was conscious, but the briefcase was trapped between the engine and the stern. With a tight knot around his wrist, he focused on untangling the rope from the engine to get loose. It was a final attempt to save the briefcase and his own life at the same time.

Brian and John stood on the hull to spot Alexis while Leo

searched around the boat. John quickly noticed something splashing near the engine. He spotted the top of Alexis's head and then jumped into the water to help him.

Within a few seconds, he found Alexis and understood that the rope was caught around the engine. Leo also found Alexis and dived down to help raise his head above water. As a result, Alexis was able to get one deep breath before his head was completely submerged again. The boat was slowly sinking into the deep, and it was pulling Alexis down with it.

Brian knew there was little time to act and jumped in the water. But instead of helping the others with Alexis, he swam under the boat and opened the center console's compartment door. He reached inside and grabbed the emergency raft before pulling the inflation chord. The raft shot to the surface and took form.

Alexis tried to stay calm, but he could not hold his breath for much longer. The suitcases were stuck tightly against the stern, and the boat was sinking faster by the second. Leo was also struggling to breathe and swam to the surface to take a final breath.

"Alex, you gotta let that shit go!" he yelled before going back underwater.

John tried with all his might to pull out the briefcase until he swallowed water and started choking, forcing him to swim up for air. Brian was already on the raft and tossed a rope to John. Then he jumped into the water to try and help Leo.

But it was too late. The boat lost its buoyancy. It pointed the bow upwards and drug the Garcia brothers into the darkness of the Atlantic Ocean.

"Let go!" yelled Brian as he held on to the raft. "Let go!"

He saw the last of his father's boat disappear and looked for any sign of Alexis or Leo. But they were nowhere to be seen. Meanwhile, John was nearly unconscious in the raft. He had swallowed a lot of water. Brian felt helpless and started to think that his friends were dead.

The current was quickly pushing him and John further east, creating a hopeless expectation of finding the Garcia brothers. The wind howled fiercely as though claiming victory for the lives lost at sea.

Brian tried looking everywhere but mainly focused on the area where the boat had sunk. John eventually came to his senses and dragged his torso over the edge of the raft to help Brian search for Alexis and Leo.

"They're gone... shit, John, they're gone," said an exhausted Brian after getting back in the raft.

"No... they're not... look," mumbled John as he pointed at two heads floating in the water.

"Oh shit, it's them!" said Brian. He dove into the water, held the raft's rope in his teeth, and started swimming toward the brothers. John rolled off the raft and started kicking on the opposite side to help Brian. Twenty meters away, Leo was holding Alexis and swimming toward Brian and John.

"C'mon, little dude, we're almost there. So, don't die, you little shit," said Leo with tears in his eyes.

Both parties struggled to close the distance, especially Brian and John, who were swimming against the current. The effort exhausted all their energy. At times, they would advance a considerable distance, but then a wave would push them farther apart.

But Leo refused to quit fighting. He knew that Alexis needed some type of resuscitation and did not stop until they finally reached the raft.

"I can't believe you're here...," gasped Brian as he put his arm around Leo.

"We gotta see if he's okay," replied Leo about his brother.

John jumped in the raft to help pull up Alexis. Then Leo got inside, followed by Brian. They rolled Alexis on his back to observe his state.

"He's not breathing. He took in a lot of water... Fuck!" expressed a frantic Leo.

He didn't hesitate to slap his brother two times on the face before attempting air resuscitation. He pinched his brother's nose and proceeded to blow air into his lungs. He stopped and started to pump on Alexis's chest. After ten seconds of pumping, he returned to blowing air into his lungs. After receiving no response, Leo started yelling at his little brother.

"Come the fuck on, you pussy! Wake the fuck up!"

John and Brian looked on with fear. After a few more shakes, Leo continued to blow air into Alexis's lungs. And just as all hope was lost, Alexis started coughing up water. Leo, John, and Brian turned him on his belly to help let the water out of his lungs. Alexis continued to cough out water, mucous, and vomit.

"Get rid of all that shit, bro," said John as he patted Alexis's back.

After catching his breath, Alexis turned around and stared at the sky. Leo collapsed next to his brother and put his arm around him.

"You fucking scared me, you little shit. I knew we should've never done this shit," he complained.

"I'm good, bro... I'm good," replied a depleted Alexis. "We saw you go down. What happened? How'd you get out?" asked John.

"We went down, but I kept pulling the rope. The briefcase handles finally broke, and we were able to get loose. Alexis was unconscious, so I grabbed him and swam to the top," replied Leo, who was still trying to catch his breath.

"So, what about the money?" asked Brian. John was also eager to hear the status of the loot.

"It's gone. As soon as the handle broke off the briefcase, it all went to the bottom of the ocean," revealed Leo.

The news was almost unbearable to accept, despite their gratefulness for being alive. They had failed to complete the heist. In the end, it was all for nothing. And with no certainty of getting rescued, it also seemed likely they were going to die at sea.

Everybody closed their eyes and allowed fate to dictate their future. They slept for hours until John was the first to awaken. He noticed a buzzing sound in the distance and raised his head to investigate. There were two fishing boats cruising to a destination. So, John raised his arms and yelled as loud as he could.

"Hey! Over here! Over here!"

That woke up the others, even Alexis. Brian and Leo became

aware of the situation and also yelled for help. They yelled, and yelled, and yelled, and waived their arms in the air. Luckily for the boys, a privileged child on one of the boats noticed the commotion. He notified his mother, who notified her husband.

"Mark, I think those people need help," said the woman. The husband decelerated and used his binoculars to get a better view. As soon as he confirmed that the boys were in distress, he turned the wheel and accelerated toward them. The second boat soon followed.

Once they saw the boats coming their way, Alexis said, "It was destiny, fellas. It was never meant to be." He looked at the sky and repeated, "It was never meant to be."

The large boat with four large engines circled around the raft before the captain tossed a line. Leo grabbed the rope, and they were pulled to safety. The four friends helped each other on the boat as their rescuers handed out bottles of water and food. The captain noticed their weak conditions and asked, "What happened? Did you guys get caught in the storm?"

"Yeah, we were out here fishing," replied John. "Fishing for what? Dolphin?" replied the captain. "No, for something much bigger," said John.

Chapter Twenty-One

After the captain of the boat called the coast guard to notify him about the rescue, the media outlets immediately responded. There were reporters with cameras waiting at the marina when they arrived. The rescue was blasted on every news station in South Florida as a dramatic New Year's Eve rescue. John, Alexis, Leo, and Brian had suddenly become local celebrities.

In the end, they went with the narrative. It was all nothing but a late-night fishing trip that went bad. The consequences that followed were far less severe than any of the boys expected. The Garcia brothers had to take a Spanish scolding from mama, but it was only out of love and concern. Brian, on the other hand, thought his father was going to kill him for sinking the boat. But the pending insurance check and residual payment left him with little room to complain.

Herb Bowman told the police that he suspected John and Alexis were involved in the burglary. But without clear evidence and with the boy's alibi, the police had no reason to pursue them. Herb received insurance money for the card and damages. But without the Honus Wagner T206, he no longer stood on top of the sports collectibles world. It was a debilitating and devaluating loss for him.

There wasn't much commotion at John's house about the incident. He went home and rested for a week before emerging from his room. All the while, he didn't have a single cigarette. He not only used the time to heal his body but his mind as well. The scare that he experienced in that ocean helped put his entire life in perspective. Although he loved his family more than anything,

John no longer wanted to bear their shortcomings, their depression, and their anger.

Shannon quickly found out about the fishing accident. She immediately tried to contact John through phone calls and text messages, but he never replied. In his time of isolation and healing, he thought a lot about her. He mostly thought of ways that he could be a better person for her. But she didn't know this and was left to think that he was ignoring her for other reasons. She stopped calling after three days of trying.

When the week was over, John left the house for his first day of work since the heist. Before leaving the parking lot of his apartment complex, he brought out a trash bag and cleaned the piles of garbage in the front and back seats of his car. Then he stepped into the old Escort, put the key in the ignition, and turned on the car on the first attempt. John took a deep breath to absorb the car's familiar scent. He was grateful for the new day that presented a new opportunity to live a life of peace.

As usual, Vincent was just getting home after a night of partying. John had the window down, so he walked up to talk to his big brother.

"What's up, man? Going to work?" asked Vincent.

"Yep, first day back," replied John. "Where were you last night?" he asked.

"I went to the Heat game with some co-workers. We all pitched in for a room at the Fountain Blue and went there after," replied Vincent. "You alright?"

"Yeah, bro. I feel fucking great," expressed John.

"I'm glad... and uh... I just wanted to tell you that I'm sorry. I'm going to try a lot harder to help you take care of Mom and Dad. I promise," said Vincent.

Those words melted John's heart. He had to hold back from crying. His tranquility was only altered by Vincent's honest revelation.

"I'll see you later. We should go catch a hockey game with Dad this week," replied John before putting on his shades and pulling out of the parking space.

He drove to Alexis's house before work to check up on him. They hadn't spoken since the boat sunk, and he wanted to see if Alexis had recovered well. To no surprise, he drove up to the garage and found Alexis hitting the punching bag for a morning workout.

Alexis saw John step out of the car and walk towards the garage. He stopped throwing vicious combinations and turned to address his friend.

"We almost fucking had it, John," said Alexis.

"I know, bro. Trust me, I know," replied John.

"Everything now feels like it was a dream. Planning that shit, breaking in, the boat ride, Mrs. Loretta... it was nothing more than a dream," said Alexis.

"I've been thinking about this too. It's okay. We were never meant to have that money, Alexis. Like Mrs. Loretta said, it was destiny. We were only supposed to bring her back that card. It belonged to her and not that shyster...," said John.

"I don't know... I guess I'm just more upset that the plan wasn't completed. I hate failure," said Alexis.

At that point, Leo walked through the garage and towards his truck. John was surprised to see him awake and active so early in the morning.

"Whoa, where you going to so early?" asked John. "Culinary school... now get the fuck out of my way," replied Leo as he walked through John. The boys saw him step into his truck and drive away.

"I need to get ready for class too… don't want to miss the first day. But I'm glad we did this, my friend. Even though we didn't get the cash, I know it wasn't all in vain. And if an opportunity like this ever presents itself again, you know I always have your back," said Alexis.

John left the Garcia estate and drove to work. The only other person he wanted to see was Shannon. He was certain that she was going to be there. He didn't want to waste another minute of his life without her by his side. After absorbing the magnitude of everything that'd happened, John came to a single, life-altering conclusion. It was Shannon's love, not the money, that brought him all the peace and happiness in the world.

He parked the car in one of the usual spaces and stepped out without his morning routine. He wasn't high, and he didn't smell of weed and cigarettes. John simply tucked his buttoned shirt into his khakis and proceeded to find Shannon.

As soon as he entered the store, all the other employees, including Angelica, looked at him like he was a ghost. Everyone knew about the boat accident, but they didn't know when to expect him back at work, if ever. The only person who knew was Tanisha.

John found Shannon sorting and organizing the magazine section. She also had no idea that he was returning to work. He stood behind her as she marked which magazines were out of stock.

"Shannon," said John, catching her completely off guard.

Shannon recognized his voice and turned around to look at him. She'd spent the entire week frozen in a single state of mind, worried if they would ever see each other again. She didn't know whether to scold him or kiss him. But after looking into his eyes and sensing that an explanation wasn't necessary, she let her guard down. John approached Shannon, gave her a kiss on the lips, and they held each other for a minute as customers and co-workers watched.

THE END

About the Author

Fabian Hernandez is an American author. The son of immigrants, he was born in Louisiana and grew up in South Florida. He's earned a Bachelor's degree in Humanities and a Master's degree in Biomedical Sciences. Fabian combines his imagination, his attention to detail, and his love for the English language to create unique and compelling stories.